LINCOLNSHIRE PEOPLE

Compiled by

John R. Ketteringham

Terence Leach (1937–1994)

LINCOLNSHIRE PEOPLE

Compiled by
John R. Ketteringham

The King's England Press
1995

Dedicated with gratitude to the memory of Terence R. Leach (1937–1994) whose knowledge of Lincolnshire people and places was unrivalled.

First published in 1995 by The King's England Press,
37 Crookes Lane, Carlton, Barnsley, South Yorkshire S71 3JR.

© John Ketteringham

ISBN 1 872438 12 1

Printed and bound in Great Britain by Bookcraft (Bath) Ltd.

CONTENTS

ILLUSTRATIONS

Many people kindly lent, sent, or suggested illustrative material for this book, with the result that not all pictures could be used; nevertheless, the grateful thanks of the author and publisher go to *all* those who contributed illustrations, whether used or not. Some of the illustrations suggested, both used and unused in the book, lie in the public domain and are not therefore specifically credited here; for the remainder the author and publishers are especially grateful to the following people for the illustrations listed below

I] IN MEDALLIONS ON COVER

BANKS, Sir Joseph, portrait by Benjamin West. [Usher Gallery Lincoln]
HONYWOOD, Michael, portrait by Hannemann. [Dean and Chapter, Lincoln Cathedral]
LINLEY, Thomas, portrait by Gainsborough. [Dulwich Picture Gallery]
NEWTON, Sir Isaac, portrait by Sir Godfrey Kneller. [Grantham Museum]
RACE, Steve, [BBC Radio 2]
WILLOUGHBY de ERESBY, 12th Baron, 'PEREGRINE BERTIE'. [Baroness Willoughby de Eresby]

II] FRONTISPIECE

LEACH, Terence, b/w print. [*Lincs Echo*]

III] INTEGRATED WITH TEXT

CAPES, Geoff, b/w print. [Geoff Capes]
CHAPLIN, Henry, *Spy* Cartoon, reproduced from original in the possession of John Smith. [John Smith]
CHESHIRE, Leonard, b/w print. [The Leonard Cheshire Foundation and Brian Aris, photographer]
CULLEN, Alex, b/w print. [Alex Cullen]
DASHWOOD, Francis [Dunston Pillar], b/w print, c. 1940. [Lincolnshire Libraries]
DYMOKES [The], b/w print of the Lion Gate at Scrivelsby. [John Ketteringham]
HILL, Sir Francis, b/w print of original in possession of Philip Race. [Philip Race]
HILTON, William, RA, b/w print of self portrait. [credit Usher Gallery Lincoln]
INGRAM, H., Statue, b/w print. [Hilary Healey]
KING, Edward, Bishop, b/w print. [Collection of the late Terence Leach]
LOGSDAIL, William, self portrait. [Usher Gallery Lincoln]
MAKINS, EDWARD, 'TORKSEY NED', b/w contemporary postcard. [Robert Sutton Collection]
MARRINER, Sir Neville, b/w print. [Sir Neville Marriner]
PAINE, Tom, portrait. [Windmill Hotel, Alford]
SWYNFORD, Katherine, line drawing by David Vale of tombs in Swyneford Chantry. [Dean and Chapter, Lincoln Cathedral]
TENNYSON, Alfred, Lord, b/w postcard dtd. 1905 showing the Watts statue of Tennyson in the Cathedral Precincts. [Robert Sutton Collection]
THATCHER, Margaret [Baroness Thatcher], b/w print. [Baroness Thatcher]
TWIGG, John, b/w print of Twigg in the stocks at Alford.[*Lincs Echo*]
VARAH, Chad, b/w print. [*Lincs Echo*]
WILLIS, Francis, portrait. [Usher Gallery Lincoln]
WINN, Henry, contemporary photograph. [Lincs County Council]
WINT, Peter de, charcoal sketch. [Usher Gallery Lincoln]

FOREWORD

Every county must have its catalogue of characters, its list of people who have made a significant contribution to life - in religion, science, politics, exploration, the arts, sport, serving their county in war, and even in gaining notoriety. Lincolnshire can certainly claim an honourable and lengthy list. Some names of the past - Banks, Franklin, Newton, Tennyson and Wesley - should be well known. But who were Colley Cibber, George Boole, Tommy Lidgett and Sarah Swift? To find out, you would need to do a deal of delving.

Some of the sources, apart from full biographies of the best known (and the *Dictionary of National Biography*, of course), were *Lincolnshire in History and Lincolnshire Worthies* (1903), around 550 short biographies in *Lincolnshire at the Opening of the Twentieth Century* (1907), and over 830 in *Who's Who in Lincolnshire* (1935). Others were to be found in the short-lived county magazine the *Lincolnshire Poacher* (1900-1901), and when I was editor of *Lincolnshire Life* we published a series of *Sixty Lincolnshire Worthies* in the 1980s; and the magazine has always, since it first appeared in 1961, had a 'Personality of the Month'

Now, with the publication of this volume of short biographies, you have a ready reference. The term 'Lincolnshire Worthies' implies people from the past. From these, John Ketteringham has made his own selection to cover as wide a range in time and types as possible. But he has also gone a step further by including a smattering of living personalities. There is much to interest, even surprise. I hope you enjoy it.

David N. Robinson
Former Editor, *Lincolnshire Life*
Louth, September 1994

INTRODUCTION AND ACKNOWLEDGEMENTS

There are many natives of the historic county of Lincolnshire who have achieved international fame, such as Tennyson and the Wesley brothers, but there are also many others, who, although not natives of the county, have become well-known because of their achievements in Lincolnshire. These include such well-known people as Group Captain Leonard Cheshire V. C. and Billy Butlin, the holiday camp pioneer. There are those characters such as Dick Turpin the highwayman and Haigh the acid bath murderer, whose time spent in the county had certain consequences for them.

I have long felt that a collection of short biographies of such people would be a useful addition to the literature of Lincolnshire and this offering is a hotchpotch of all those who, for one reason or another, I have felt should be included. Although the final choice is very much my own, I am grateful to all those, too numerous to mention individually, who suggested likely people for inclusion and I am sure readers will have their own favourites whom I have overlooked. I would be pleased to hear about them.

For those readers who would like more information about any of the personalities I have, wherever possible, suggested further reading. The *Dictionary of National Biography* is also a useful source.

I acknowledge the assistance of those who read the text in part or in its entirety and made suggestions or corrections. Of course, any errors which remain are my own responsibility and I hope readers will not hesitate to let me know about them.

Permission to reproduce portraits, photographs and other illustrations was given readily by a number of people and I acknowledge the following:

Baroness Willoughby de Eresby for the portrait of Peregrine Bertie; the Dean and Chapter of Lincoln Cathedral for the portrait of Michael Honywood and for the reconstruction of the Swyneford Chantry drawn by David Vale; Dulwich Picture Gallery for the portrait of Thomas Linley Jnr. The *Lincolnshire Echo* gave permission for me to use the photographs of Terence Leach and Rev. Dr. Chad Varah. Mr John Smith gave permission for me to use the Spy cartoon of Henry Chaplin. I am grateful to Philip Race for permission to use the photograph of Sir Francis Hill. Lincolnshire County Council (The Usher Gallery, Lincoln) gave me permission to use the illustrations of Sir Joseph Banks, William Hilton, William Logsdail, Alfred, Lord Tennyson, Francis Willis and Peter de Wint. Grantham Museum gave me permission to use the portrait of Sir Isaac Newton. The photograph of Thomas Paine was supplied by the *Lincolnshire Echo*, from a portrait at the Windmill Hotel, Alford, who gave me permission to reproduce it. All those people in the book who are thankfully still living readily sent me photographs of themselves.

I do hope all those friends who have helped and encouraged me in the production of this book whom I have not named individually will accept my thanks and I hope that they enjoy the result.

John R. Ketteringham
Lincoln, 1994

Christopher ADDISON (1869-1951)

Christopher Addison was born at Willow Farm Hogsthorpe on 19 June 1869 and was educated at Magdalene College School, Wainfleet, and Trinity College Harrogate. After graduating from University College Sheffield he went on to the Medical School at St. Bartholomew's Hospital, London. After filling a number of hospital appointments he was elected Member of Parliament as a Liberal for the Hoxton constituency from 1910 to 1922. In 1929 he was elected to Parliament as a member of the Labour Party for the Swindon constituency but lost the seat in 1931, regaining it in 1934.

During his parliamentary career Addison held a large number of ministerial posts including Minister for Munitions from 1915 to 1917 and Minister for Reconstruction in 1917. In 1919 he became the first Minister of Health and remained in that post until 1921. He is best known to many for the Addison standard for early council houses which was introduced during his Ministry. Amongst other posts he held during his Parliamentary career were Parliamentary Secretary to the Board of Education, Minister of Agriculture and Paymaster General.

Christopher Addison was responsible for a large number of publications both medical and political. He was created Baron Addison of Stallingborough in 1937 and became a Viscount in 1945. Lord Addison died on 11 December 1951.

Henry ANDREWS (1743-1820)

Henry Andrews was born at Freiston in 1743 and at the age of ten began observing the stars with a telescope mounted on a table. He quickly developed a fondness for astronomical observations. Young Henry entered domestic service in the house of a shopkeeper in Sleaford and later moved to Lincoln where he worked for a Mr. Verinum, who greatly encouraged his studies. On 1 April 1764, a distinguished company gathered at Aswarby Hall was able to view an eclipse of the sun which Andrews had calculated with great accuracy.

He became an usher at a school kept by a clergyman at Stilton before moving to Cambridge and finally setting up as a bookseller in Royston, Hertfordshire, where he remained until his death on 26 January 1820. For more than forty years he was one of the calculators for the *Nautical Almanack* and was also employed by Moore's and other almanacks.

Anne ASKEW (1521-46)

One of the bravest of Lincolnshire women, Anne Askew was born at Stallingborough in 1521 and was the daughter of Sir William Askew or Ascough. Anne was highly educated and a serious student of the bible who was able to form her own opinions seeing both the rights and wrongs of traditional religious beliefs. She was prepared to fight against these wrongs, as many of the clergy of Lincoln Cathedral found when they tried to argue with her. A marriage was arranged for Anne's eldest sister to Thomas Kyme of Friskney but the bride-to-be died and to avoid financial loss Anne was offered as substitute.

Although she bore her husband two children, Anne eventually left him to go to London. It has been said that her brother Francis, whose monument is to be seen in Stallingborough church, betrayed her religious principles and she was in danger of arrest but it may be that her religious views so offended the local clergy that she was forced to join other Protestant reformers in London.

London was torn apart by religious discord and Anne spoke out boldly against transubstantiation and other dogmas of the old faith. She was in communication with many ladies of the Court including Catherine Parr, the sixth and last wife of Henry VIII, who was an active supporter of reform. Anne was charged with heresy and in March 1545 she appeared before the Lord Mayor of London and the infamous Bishop Bonner who is said to have sent two hundred Protestants to the stake. Anne was not intimidated and the Bishop tried to befriend her but she would not be persuaded and all attempts to make her deny her beliefs failed. She continued to preach against the establishment and within a year she had been arrested and indicted again for heresy. This time there was no escape and she was committed to Newgate and given a final chance to recant. She refused and was moved to the Tower where she was questioned about her association with Catherine Parr. Torture failed to obtain a confession and such was her condition after this ordeal that she had to be carried to the stake at Smithfield. Even while the flames were inflicting more pain on her she contradicted the Catholic prayers being read by the clergy. Anne was aged twenty-five when she died in 1546.

FURTHER READING: Wilson, D. *Tudor Tapestry* (1972)

Joseph BANKS (1743-1820)

Joseph Banks was born in London on 13 February 1744 and was the only son of William Banks of Revesby Abbey. His early education was by a private tutor and at the age of nine he was sent to Harrow. When he reached the age of thirteen he transferred to Eton and whilst there he became interested in botany. He was greatly influenced by a copy of Gerard's *Herbal* which he found in the library at Revesby. Banks went up to Christ Church College, Oxford in 1760 where his interest in botany increased and he also became interested in other branches of the natural sciences. He was influential in obtaining a lecturer in Botany for the University.

In 1766 he was elected a fellow of the Royal Society and in the same year voyaged to Newfoundland collecting plants. Between 1768 and 1771 he accompanied Captain James Cook's expedition round the world. In 1772 he visited the Hebrides and Iceland and in 1778 he was elected President of the Royal Society, an office which he held for 41 years. In 1781 Joseph Banks was created a baronet and in 1795 he was invested with the Order of the Bath. He was created a Privy Councillor in 1797. Banks founded the African Association and the colony of New South Wales owes its origin to him.

When he died on 19 June 1820 he bequeathed his library and herbarium to his librarian, who gave them to the British Museum. Although Sir Joseph was a somewhat autocratic man, he was able to use his wealth and influence for the benefit and advancement of scientific exploration. It was his patronage of science rather than the actual work which he did himself which was of such great importance.

FURTHER READING: Carter, H. B. *Sir Joseph Banks 1743-1820* (1988)

George BASS (1771-?1812)

The discoverer of Bass Strait was born at Aswarby near Sleaford in 1771 and was the son of a farmer. On the death of his father the family moved to Boston and, although young George had always wanted to go to sea, his mother persuaded him to become apprenticed to a surgeon in that town. After qualifying in London he was appointed surgeon on board HMS *Reliance.*

The *Reliance* sailed for Botany Bay in 1795 and Lincolnshire-born Matthew Flinders was also a member of the crew. Bass purchased a small whaling boat in order to explore the coast of New South Wales and realised that a sea-passage existed which in the following year he explored in a sloop commanded by Lieutenant Flinders. This sea passage has ever since been known as 'Bass Strait'. He continued to circumnavigate Tasmania which was thus proved to be an island.

Because of ill health George Bass retired from the Navy and left Australia in 1799 to return to England. He returned to Australia in 1801 with a cargo of food and then sailed on to Tahiti to purchase more food before returning to Sydney. In February 1803 Bass set sail for South America and little more is known of him. Several sightings in South America were reported from time to time and he is assumed to have died in South America in 1812.

Peregrine BERTIE (1550-1601)

Richard Bertie and his wife Catherine Baroness Willoughby de Eresby fled from their home in Spilsby to the continent to escape the Marian religious persecutions and their son, Peregrine, was born in a cottage in Wessel, Germany. The family had to be continually on the move in order to escape capture but eventually found safety in Poland where they remained until the death of Queen Mary.

Peregrine married the daughter of the Earl of Oxford and when his mother died he became the tenth Lord Willoughby de Eresby. He undertook a number of missions on behalf of Queen Elizabeth and he joined the Earl of Leicester's army against the Spaniards. In 1586 he became military governor of Bergen-op-Zoom and soon after was responsible for capturing a large Spanish convoy bound for Antwerp.

In 1587 Lord Willoughby became commander of the English forces in the Netherlands. The army was badly equipped and he was ordered to negotiate a peace with the Spaniards but this was unsuccessful. He continued to fight bravely against the Spaniards with some success but in 1589 returned home in poor health having spent much of his own money to provide for his army. Later in the same year he was sent to France with an army of 4,000 men to assist Henry of Navarre but again the army was ill-equipped and suffered greatly. In 1590 the remnants of the army returned to England.

Peregrine Bertie was appointed Governor of Berwick-on-Tweed where he remained for the remainder of his life. He was buried in the Willoughby Chapel in St. James's Church, Spilsby.

Henry of BOLINGBROKE (1367-1413)

The future King Henry IV was born at Bolingbroke Castle on 3 April 1367 and is the only King known to have been born in Lincolnshire. Henry of Bolingbroke, as he was often known, was the son of John of Gaunt and his mother was a daughter of Henry, Duke of Lancaster. At the age of ten Henry was created a Knight of the Garter by Edward III and three months later he carried a sword at the Coronation of Richard II. In the same year, 1377, he was styled Earl of Derby and when a year later John of Gaunt was overseas young Henry was appointed 'warden of the regality of the Palatine County of Lancaster'. Richard II became unpopular because of his favourites and Henry was one of those opposed to the King. However, Henry appears to have remained quietly at Bolingbroke until 1395 when he was one of a Council appointed to rule England while Richard II was in Ireland.

In 1397 Henry was created Duke of Hereford and in the following year as the result of a quarrel with the Duke of Norfolk he was banished for ten years. In 1399 the banishment was made permanent and Henry's estates were confiscated. In the July of that year Henry landed at Ravenspur near Withernsea and quickly gathered a large following particularly from the North. The King was captured but Henry insisted that he was only concerned to claim his inheritance. However, on 29 September 1399 the King renounced the Crown and Henry was chosen by Parliament to be his successor. He was crowned on 13 October 1399. Henry IV died on 20 March 1413 and was buried in Canterbury Cathedral.

FURTHER READING: Kirby, J. L. *Henry IV, King of England* (1970)

John BOLLE (died 1606)

Sir John Bolle of Thorpe Hall near Louth was knighted by Queen Elizabeth I after the expedition against Cadiz in 1596 in which he distinguished himself with great gallantry. However, Sir John is remembered less for his warlike deeds than for his steadfast determination not to be ensnared by the wiles of a wealthy Spanish beauty. Among the prisoners taken at Cadiz was a beautiful and wealthy Spanish lady and Sir John treated her with every courtesy and kindness. The poor lady threw herself at her captor's feet, offered him all her riches, and begged him to take her back to England, disguised as his page. Sir John told her of his wife in England and the Spanish lady realised that he would remain faithful. However, she loaded him with presents to take home to his wife including a quantity of jewels and other valuables, a tapestry bed and several casks full of plate, money and other treasures. She then became a nun!

Among the treasure which Sir John brought back to Thorpe Hall was a portrait of the lady herself, wearing a rich green dress. A tradition became established that the Hall was haunted by a lady dressed in green, who sat every night under a particular tree near the mansion. So seriously did the family take this haunting that, during the lifetime of Sir John's heir, Charles Bolle, a place was always laid at the dinner table for the Green Lady, in case she should choose to appear! The legend must have taken deep hold on the imagination of the people of the time for a long ballad was written about the episode entitled *The Spanish lady's love for an Englishman*.

George BOOLE (1815-1864)

George Boole was born on 2 November 1815 and was the son of a tradesman in Lincoln. He was educated at elementary schools in Lincoln but his father had some ability as a mechanic and in elementary mathematics which must have been of some assistance to young George.

At the age of sixteen he was employed as a teacher in Lincoln and then at a school in Waddington. At the age of twenty, he opened a school on his own account but devoted all his spare time to the study of Greek, Latin, French, German and Italian. His interest in mathematics appears to have developed later in life and in 1849 he was appointed to the mathematics chair in the newly founded Queen's College in Cork where he spent the remainder of his life.

George Boole became public examiner for degrees at Queen's University and was awarded the Royal Society's Medal in 1844 and the Keith Medal by the Royal Society of Edinburgh in 1857. The degrees of Doctor of Law and Doctor of Civil Law were conferred on him by Dublin and Oxford Universities respectively.

Boole is best known for applying algebraic symbolism to logical procedures and was the inventor of Boolean algebra. His best known book was published in 1854 and is entitled *An investigation of the laws of thought in which are founded the mathematical theories of logic and probabilities.* Boole wrote two mathematical textbooks and a considerable number of papers which were published in various mathematical and other journals. He died suddenly on 8 December 1864.

FURTHER READING: MacHale, D. *George Boole, his life and work* (Dublin, 1985)
Barry, P. D, (Ed.) *George Boole: A Miscellany* (Cork, 1969)

William BOOTH (1829-1912)

The future founder of the Salvation Army, William Booth was the son of a Nottingham builder and was born on 10 April 1829. He was apprenticed to a pawnbroker in Nottingham and at an early age he came into contact with extreme poverty. When his apprenticeship came to an end at the age of nineteen he was out of work for a year and in 1849 he went to seek work in the pawnbroking trade in London.

William regularly attended the Broad Street Wesleyan Chapel in Nottingham and he preached his first sermon there at the age of seventeen. He devoted all his spare-time to preaching and in 1852 he became a minister in the Methodist Church. In November of the same year, at the age of twenty-three, William Booth was appointed to the Spalding circuit of the Wesleyan Reform Movement.

He spent much time preaching in the Fenlands and in December of the following year he was invited to lead a crusade in the Caistor area. This was so successful that he was asked to spend another week at Caistor in January of the following year and he returned again in the February. His experience at this time moved him greatly and, had he not already arranged to return to London to join the New Connexion, he might well have stayed in Lincolnshire.

On his return to Spalding, Booth spent three months in intensive study to prepare him for his ministry with the New Connexion and in June 1854 returned once again to Caistor for a rest. Unfortunately for William this was not to be, as meetings were arranged for him and although this pleased him, he resolved never again to take a rest where he was so well known!

In 1855 William Booth became a travelling evangelist in the New Connexion and in the same year married Catherine Mumford. When she was expecting their first child Catherine stayed in Caistor whilst William travelled on to Hull.

William Booth was a passionate evangelist and had an uncomplicated view of Christianity. He said that religion was a very simple thing and it just meant loving God with all one's heart and loving one's neighbours. In 1865 these principles led to the founding by William and Catherine Booth of the Christian Mission, which because of its organisation on military lines and because the Booths saw it as an 'army' of Christians fighting the evangelical cause, was re-named The Salvation Army with William as its first 'General'.

The work of 'The Army without Guns' which, as well as seeking converts to Christianity, from its inception provided food, clothing and furniture to needy people, grew rapidly. General Booth returned to Caistor in 1905 and this time the High Street was decorated with flags and bunting and large crowds gathered to welcome him. He said that it was at Caistor that he first commenced the work that was to become so dear to him. This comment clearly confirms that the time spent by the founder of the Salvation Army in Lincolnshire had considerable influence on him.

FURTHER READING: Begbie, Harold. *Life of William Booth* (1920)

Basil BOOTHROYD (1910-1988)

Basil Boothroyd was born on 4 March 1910 and educated at Lincoln Cathedral Choir School and the Lincoln School (now Christ's Hospital School). He began his working life as a bank clerk and was in the Royal Air Force police from 1941 to 1945. Basil Boothroyd commenced his career as a writer by contributing continuously to *Punch* from 1938 and he became Assistant Editor in 1952. He also made a considerable number of broadcasts and became well-known as a comic journalist. He was awarded the Imperial Tobacco Radio Award for the best comedy script in 1976.

Boothroyd undertook the adaptation for a television series of *The Diary of a Nobody* in 1982. He wrote a number of humorous books including *Home Guard Goings On* in 1941, *Are Officers Necessary?* (1946) and, in 1966, *You Can't Be Serious.* In 1971 he wrote the approved autobiography of the Duke of Edinburgh. His autobiography *A Shoulder To Laugh On* was published in 1987 and he died on 27 February 1988.

Robert Carr BRACKENBURY (1752-1818)

Robert Carr Brackenbury was born in 1752 at Wragby and was educated at Felstead, Essex and St. Catherine's College, Cambridge. He joined the Methodists and in 1776 he met John Wesley. As a result, he became an enthusiastic travelling preacher and was responsible for introducing Methodism to the Channel Islands.

Although never ordained, he had considerable influence on the growth of Methodism in Lincolnshire. When Brackenbury built Raithby Hall near Spilsby he also constructed a chapel over an existing stable and this was opened by John Wesley in July 1779. The chapel still survives and has recently been restored. It is the venue for the popular series of annual lectures which were inaugurated in 1980 as a memorial to Robert Carr Brackenbury. These are sponsored by the Lincolnshire Methodist History Society, the Tennyson Society and the Society for Lincolnshire History and Archaeology.

Brackenbury died on 11 August 1818 and there is a memorial to him in Raithby parish church.

FURTHER READING: Leach, T. *John Wesley's Earthly Paradise* (1993)

Gonville BROMHEAD (1844-1891)

The hero of the battle of Rorke's Drift was a member of the Lincolnshire family which has its seat at Thurlby Hall near Lincoln. Gonville was actually born at Versailles on 29 August 1844 and served with the 2nd Battalion, The 24th Regiment. He was posted to Rorke's Drift, Natal, South Africa, with 890 soldiers and he and his fellow officer, John Chard, were required to defend the post against some 4,000 Zulus. This was to prevent the invasion of Natal. The battle with the Zulus took place during the night of 22 and 23 January 1879 and the two young lieutenants used wagons, sacks of maize and biscuit boxes to create a barricade. Eventually they had to retreat to a small stone kraal where they remained overnight. To their surprise and relief the enemy disappeared during the night and reinforcements arrived to relieve them.

Lieutenants Bromhead and Chard were both awarded the Victoria Cross, together with nine of their comrades. The film *Zulu* was based on this incident with Michael Caine as Bromhead.

Lieutenant Gonville Bromhead died at Allahabad, India on 10 October 1891.

Richard BUSBY (1606-95)

Richard Busby was born in 1606 at Lutton near Long Sutton. His father was a churchwarden and his mother was the sister of Henry Robinson whose son Sir Thomas was later Treasurer of the Inner Temple. The family moved to Westminster and Richard's early education was at Westminster School. In 1624 he went up to Christ Church College, Oxford, and was awarded the degree of Bachelor of Arts in 1631. He had some ability as an actor and appeared in a play with the title *The Royal Slave*, which was performed at Christ Church before the King and Queen. However, he decided against a career on the stage and entered Holy Orders.

In 1638 Richard Busby was invited to become temporary Headmaster of Westminster School and the appointment was confirmed two years later at an annual stipend of £20 with a further £19 6s 8d in lieu of 'diet'. In addition to this he had the use of the headmaster's house. It was not long before Busby earned the reputation of being a particularly good schoolmaster.

Though he was Headmaster during the troubled time of the Civil War, the execution of King Charles I, the Interregnum, the Restoration of Charles II and Monmouth's Rebellion, Busby never wavered in his loyalty to both Crown and Church. This was recognised at the Restoration by his appointment as a Prebendary of Westminster and Treasurer of the Abbey. The degree of Doctor of Divinity was conferred on him by Oxford University and in 1661 at the Coronation of Charles II it was Busby who carried the ampulla.

Busby was proud of the fact that, during his 57 years as Headmaster of Westminster School, he produced a number of outstanding scholars. At one time sixteen Bishops owed their education to him. John Dryden, the dramatist and poet laureate, was a pupil and Richard Steele said of Busby : 'Those who passed through his instruction have such a peculiar readiness of fancy and delicacy of taste as is seldom found in men educated elsewhere. He had a power of raising what a lad had in him to the utmost height: no indifferent people came out of his hands'

Dr. Busby wrote a number of books during his long career, mostly for use in the school, but, as he never put his name to a book it is hard to be certain which were his. In 1685 he tried to devise a universal phonetic alphabet consisting of thirty-six letters to cover the sounds produced in all known languages. Busby paid for the restoration of Lutton parish church and the pulpit bearing his initials and date 1702 was erected from his bequest. Having outlived most of his relations and having remained a bachelor he left £200 for the relief of poor ministers in Lincolnshire and other counties. He made many other bequests on condition that the recipients should 'deliver thirty lectures on thirty Sundays in every year'.

FURTHER READING: Barker, G. F. R. *Memoir of Richard Busby, D.D. 1606-1695* (1895)

Billy BUTLIN (1899-1980)

William Edmund Butlin was born in South Africa but his parents moved to Canada when he was three years old and he always said that he only ever received three years' formal education.

When aged fifteen he lied about his age and enlisted as a bugle boy with the Canadian Army. He served in France during the First World War. After returning to Toronto at the end of the war he had a few jobs before deciding to join his uncle in the fairground business in England. Billy, as he was always known, worked his passage to Liverpool on a cattle boat and only had £5 with him when he landed. His uncle provided him with a hoopla stall and within a few years Billy was able to travel around the fairgrounds with his own roundabouts.

In 1927 he visited Skegness and set up an amusement park, eventually installing the first dodgem track in the British Isles. Billy realised that he had arrived at the right place at the right time and when Skegness Council decided to relocate all the amusements, he offered to build a new amusement park and pay a rental to the Council. He followed his success at Skegness by opening an amusement park at Mablethorpe.

Butlin's success was now established and he saw the advantages of providing accommodation and amusements for holiday makers all on one site. He purchased land to the north of Skegness at Ingoldmells and the country's first holiday camp opened in 1936. It had three very successful seasons until it was taken over by the Navy in 1939 as a recruit training establishment and named HMS *Royal Arthur.* Butlin opened a second camp at Clacton in 1938 and others were established eventually at Ayr, Pwllheli, Mosney (Ireland), Bognor, Minehead and Barry.

He was knighted in 1964 and his last visit to Lincolnshire was to switch on the illuminations at Skegness in 1977. Sir Billy Butlin died in his Jersey home on 12 June 1980.

FURTHER READING: Butlin, Sir Billy. *The Billy Butlin Story* (1982)

William BYRD (1543-1623)

William Byrd is believed to have been born in Lincoln in 1543 but all that is known of his early life is that he was 'bred into musick with Thomas Tallis', which suggests that some of his early life was spent in London. He was appointed organist and master of the choristers at Lincoln Cathedral on 25 March 1563 at the age of 19 or 20. On 14 September 1568 Byrd married Juliana Birley at St. Margaret's in the Close, near Lincoln Cathedral.

Even after he was appointed a gentleman of the Chapel Royal and joint organist with Thomas Tallis in 1572, he appears to have kept up his connections with Lincoln. The Dean and Chapter continued to pay a quarter of his salary in return for 'church songs' until 1581. Although Byrd conformed with the established religion he remained a Catholic at heart.

Thomas Tallis and William Byrd were granted a licence by Queen Elizabeth I on 22 January 1575 to print and sell music for a period of twenty-one years. This monopoly appears to have been quite lucrative and when Tallis died in 1585 the monopoly passed to Byrd solely. William Byrd was a prolific composer and published a number of important works. He died on 4 July 1623 and a tablet marking his place of burial was placed in Standon (Hertfordshire) church in 1923.

FURTHER READING: Fellows, E. H. *William Byrd* (Oxford 1948)

Geoff CAPES (1949-)

Geoffrey Lewis Capes was born in Holbeach on 23 August 1949 and was the sixth child of Eileen Capes and the first by her third husband. From an early age Geoff excelled at sport but at little else and at the age of six he won 7s. 6d. in the under nines race whilst wearing Wellingtons! He played soccer for the Lincolnshire Schools XI and basketball for Holbeach but he was particularly keen on cross-country running. Geoff took up weight-lifting when a club was formed in Holbeach and at the age of seventeen he demonstrated his strength when a wheel came off his van and he held it up with his left hand while he put the wheel back on with his right hand!

Geoff's early sporting activities took place at Holbeach Athletic Club, which had been founded by Tony Clay in 1949. As a youngster Geoff was full of aggression and always in trouble but Stuart Storey was able to persuade him to channel this natural aggression into competitive sport. A member of the club, Bruce McEva, had been a shot-putter in the mid-60s and he was able to teach Geoff the rudiments of throwing. When he was fifteen Steve Storey, who was a teacher at Dr. Challoner's Grammar School, Amersham, arranged for Geoff to join the School athletic team's summer tour of Germany. He was then 6' 3" tall and was rather out of place, causing some consternation when he threw the 14 lb. shot over the heads of the German judges!

After leaving school he joined his father on the agricultural gangs and once loaded twenty tons of potatoes in twenty minutes! In July 1969 Geoff Capes joined the police force and was stationed at Peterborough. In 1972 he was posted to Wittering and then to the police headquarters in Huntingdon as an instructor in physical education. The police were very supportive and allowed Geoff facilities to pursue his sporting career.

He left the police force just before the Moscow Olympics in 1976. In 1974 Geoff set new Commonwealth and British throwing records. Unfortunately, participation in a large number of minor events took its toll and he did not have the expected success in the European Championships later that year. During 1974 he had six offers of scholarships at American Universities which he refused! During his athletic career as a shot putter Geoff gained many honours, winning two Commonwealth gold medals, two European indoor medals along with numerous British titles, and competed in three Olympic games.

In 1980 he retired from amateur athletics to compete professionally in the Highland Games and television strongman competitions. Geoff was three times Britain's Strongest Man, three times European Strongest Man and twice World Strongest Man. He also won the World Highland Games five times and was seven times Scottish Highland Games champion. In 1983 Geoff won the Whitbread British Sports award for the most outstanding field athlete of the century.

Geoff Capes has appeared on numerous television shows and Christmas 1985 saw his début as an actor when he appeared as the genie of the lamp in *Aladdin* at the Civic Theatre, Halifax. Since then he has made regular pantomime appearances.

FURTHER READING: Capes, G. *Big Shot* (London, 1981)

William CECIL (1520-98)

William Cecil was the son of a prosperous south Lincolnshire landowner and was born in 1520. He was a grandson of David Cecil, who supported Henry VII at the battle of Bosworth in 1485.

William became secretary to the Duke of Somerset, who held the reins of power during the early years of the reign of Edward VI. When Somerset was replaced by the Duke of Northumberland, William Cecil became his secretary. When Edward VI died and Northumberland tried to place Lady Jane Grey on the throne, Cecil, by absenting himself from Court with a diplomatic illness, was able to continue in favour. When Elizabeth became Queen in November 1558 Cecil was made Secretary of State and Elizabeth said of him 'This Judgment I have of you, that you will not be corrupted by any manner of gifts, and that you will be faithful to the state; and that without respect to my private will, you will give me that counsel which you think best'.

In 1572 Cecil was appointed Lord Treasurer, and was raised to the peerage as Baron Burleigh. Elizabeth regarded him as 'the gravest and wisest counsellor in all Christendom' and his counsel guided her through the many crises of her long reign. In the summer of 1598 Lord Burleigh was taken ill and the queen visited him as often as she could. He died on 4 August and is buried in St. Martin's Church, Stamford, where there is a very impressive memorial.

FURTHER READING: Read, R. *Mr. Secretary Cecil and Queen Elizabeth* (1965)

Henry CHAPLIN (1841-1923)

Henry Chaplin was the son of the vicar of Ryhall near Stamford and when his uncle Charles died childless it was his nephew who inherited Blankney Hall at the age of nineteen.

Henry was a typical example of the paternalistic squires of the Victorian and Edwardian periods. He became Master of the Burton Hunt and when the Blankney Hunt was formed in 1871 he built kennels at the Hall. Chaplin had another residence in the Burghersh Chantry close by Lincoln Cathedral and it was here that the Prince of Wales (later Edward VII) was a frequent guest.

In August 1863 the marriage had been arranged between Henry Chaplin and Lady Florence Paget, the youngest daughter of the Marquis of Angelsey. Two weeks before the intended wedding Lady Florence married Henry Hastings, the fourth Marquis of Hastings, at St. George's Church, Hanover Square, London which was, at that time, a notorious 'marriage shop' for eloping couples! The first Henry Chaplin knew of this was in a letter which had been left for him at Blankney Hall.

Ironically, Hastings' lifestyle led to his death at the age of twenty-six after Chaplin had married Lady Florence Leveson-Gower, the elder daughter of the Duke of Sutherland. Unfortunately she died five years later after bearing their third child.

In 1868 Chaplin became Member of Parliament for mid-Lincolnshire and held the seat for thirty-eight years, when he was defeated by the Liberal candidate. However, in a by-election he was elected to represent Wimbledon where his Radical opponent was Bertrand Russell. In 1916 he was created Viscount Chaplin of St. Oswald's, Blankney. When he died in 1923 *The Times* said in his obituary 'He had a sunny nature which no clouds could dim'.

Edward Parker CHARLESWORTH
(1783-1853)

Dr. Charlesworth introduced revolutionary new techniques in the treatment of the mentally ill. He was the son of the rector of Ossington, Nottinghamshire, and was a pupil of Dr. E. Harrison of Horncastle. Charlesworth went to the Medical School of Edinburgh University and graduated as a Doctor of Medicine in 1807. He married the daughter of Dr. Rocber of Horncastle and settled in Lincoln, where he acquired a large practice.

In 1808 Dr Charlesworth was appointed physician to Lincoln County Hospital which was then in Drury Lane. The building still survives as the Theological College. From its opening in 1820 he was visiting physician to the Lincoln Asylum for the Insane on Union Road which, since 1884, has been known as The Lawn. Dr Charlesworth for many years devoted himself to improving the treatment of the mentally ill. He forbade the use of restraint or violence wherever possible and eventually all forms of mechanical restraint were abolished completely.

Charlesworth was also very concerned with the welfare of the poor and soon after his death from paralysis on 20 December 1853 a statue, which still stands, was erected in the south-east corner of the grounds of the Hospital.

Leonard CHESHIRE (1917-1992)

Geoffrey Leonard Cheshire was born on 7 September 1917 and educated at Stowe School and Merton College, Oxford, graduating in 1939. He joined the Oxford University Air Squadron in 1936 and was commissioned in the Royal Air Force immediately after his graduation.

Leonard Cheshire served in Bomber Command from 1940 to 1945, rising to the rank of Group Captain. In 1943 Cheshire assumed command of 617 Squadron, having dropped a rank from Group Captain at his own request, to lead this distinguished squadron. At this time he was 25 years of age, the youngest man of that rank in the service. Having completed 100 operations while in command of 617 Squadron he was awarded the Victoria Cross. He was the official British observer at the dropping of the Atom Bomb on Nagasaki in 1945. In addition to the Victoria Cross, he was decorated with the Distinguished Service Order with two bars and the Distinguished Flying Cross.

After he retired from the Royal Air Force in December 1945 he founded the Cheshire Homes for the Disabled and 270 of these now exist. Cheshire was awarded the Order of Merit in 1981 and he, together with his wife, Sue Ryder, who also established a Foundation for the Sick and Disabled, involved themselves in a number of charitable causes. In 1991 Cheshire was created a life peer taking the title Baron Cheshire of Woodhall in the county of Lincoln.

Lord Cheshire died in August 1992 and a memorial service attended by his widow, Sue Ryder, and by the Duke of Gloucester, representing the Royal Family, was held in Lincoln Cathedral on 1 November 1992.

FURTHER READING: Owen, R. J. *Mission for a pilot: the story of Leonard Cheshire* (1980)

Wing Commander Leonard Cheshire VC, DSO, DFC

Colley CIBBER (1671-1757)

Colley Cibber was born in 1671 and was the son of a Danish born sculptor. His Christian name Colley was the maiden name of his mother, Jane Colley, who came from Glaston, Rutland. Colley said of his early education at the King's School Grantham that 'in the year 1682 at a little more than ten years of age I was sent to the Free School of Grantham in Lincolnshire where I staid till I got through it from the lowest Form to the uppermost...' At school the young Colley impressed his schoolmaster with the quality of a funeral oration which he wrote on the death of Charles II. For this he was made head of the form and for the Coronation he produced an Ode for which the school was awarded a day's holiday!

Colley Cibber joined the army for a short time before going on the stage. He made a successful appearance in Congreve's *Double Dealer* and he appeared in his own plays *Careless Husband* and *Love's Last Shift*, which were staged at Drury Lane in 1704. He became actor manager at Drury Lane, retiring at the age of 74 in 1745. His autobiography, published in 1740, is an important record of life in the eighteenth century. Rather surprisingly Colley Cibber was appointed Poet Laureate by George II in 1730. Most of his official odes were ridiculed but his poem *The Blind Boy* has survived. Colley Cibber died in London at the age of 86.

Thomas COOPER (1805-92)

Thomas Cooper was born in Leicestershire on 20 March 1805 and was the son of a dyer. When his father died in 1809, Cooper with his mother and half-sister moved to Gainsborough, where he lived for the next 24 years. Young Thomas, who was interested in music, drawing and collecting flowers, worked as a shoemaker. He became an avid reader, mainly of historical and theological works, and he even taught himself Latin, Greek and French.

In 1828, Cooper opened a fee-paying school mainly for the children of the farmers and customs men of Gainsborough. He remained a schoolmaster for the next eight years. At the same time, he became a Wesleyan Local Methodist preacher but in 1833 he left Gainsborough and went to live in Lincoln, breaking off his connection with the Methodists. A year later he married Susanna Chaloner but there were no children of the marriage.

In Lincoln, Cooper taught Latin and French at the Mechanics' Institute but when he was unsuccessful in obtaining the curator's post in 1835 he severed his connections with the Institute. He became director, secretary and treasurer of the Choral Society but his failure to consult brought about discord and in 1837 he resigned. In 1833 Cooper published, by subscription, the *Wesleyan Chiefs* and about 400 copies were printed. At the same time he began work on a novel entitled *Captain Cobbler*.

Between 1836 and 1838 he was a somewhat controversial correspondent for the *Lincoln, Rutland and Stamford Mercury*. In 1839 he moved to London and became editor of the *Kentish Mercury, Gravesend Journal and Greenwich Gazette*. In 1841 Cooper was again on the

move, this time to Leicester, where he became an ardent champion of the local Chartists. For a short time he was reporter for the *Leicestershire Mercury* and when he was dismissed he became editor of the *Midland Counties Illuminator*. This publication ran to thirteen issues and was succeeded by the *Chartist Rushlight* and the *Exterminator*.

Cooper's enthusiasm and his desire to take over the leadership of the Chartist Movement in Leicestershire led to difficulties with the old established leaders. His breakaway so-called Shakespearean Association rapidly grew to a membership of 2,500.

Cooper was given a two year prison sentence for 'seditious conspiracy'. After his release from prison he returned to London and in 1847 became a founder member of the People's International League, which was a group of radical-minded individuals. He became president of the People's Charter Union and wrote many pamphlets and articles in support of the Chartist cause. This brought him in contact with Thomas Carlyle, Charles Kingsley and Charles Dickens.

Cooper was a popular lecturer, travelling throughout England to talk on history, literature and religion. In August 1845 Cooper's greatest work was published; *Purgatory of Suicides*. This had been written whilst he was in prison and was recognized at the time as an extraordinary piece of writing. The high point of Cooper's life, and most significant, was his re-conversion to Christianity in 1858 which he confirmed publicly after surviving a train crash! He was baptized by total immersion in Friar Lane Chapel, Leicester, in 1859. From this time onwards he lectured only on Christianity. Since his Gainsborough days he had been something of a sceptic and this had been reflected in his London lectures.

Cooper continued with his work as a Christian lecturer until the early 1880s and after his retirement returned to Lincoln. Despite deteriorating health, Cooper wrote *Thoughts of Fourscore*, which expressed displeasure at most of the changes which had taken place during his life.

He died in July 1892 at the age of 87 and was buried in Lincoln. Plans by Leicester Socialists to erect a statue came to nothing but the Thomas Cooper Memorial Baptist Chapel in St Benedict's Square, Lincoln, which had been dedicated to his honour during his lifetime, remained in use until a few years ago when a replacement chapel was erected on the site of the Hannah Memorial Chapel in Lincoln's High Street.

FURTHER READING: Saville, J. *The life of Thomas Cooper* (1971)

Alexander Lamb CULLEN (1920-   )

Alexander Cullen was born on 30 April 1920 and was the son of Richard and Jessie Cullen. He attended Lincoln School (now Christ's Hospital School), where he became friendly with Steve Race and they formed a jazz duo with Alex on the drums and Steve at the piano. Unfortunately for Steve the partnership ceased when the future Professor Cullen became more interested in science than music!

Alex Cullen went on to the City and Guilds College, London and after graduating with a degree in electrical engineering he joined the staff of the Radio Department at the Royal Aircraft Establishment Farnborough. Under Dr. H. M. Barlow, he was involved during the war in work on the development and introduction of microwave radar. He remained at Farnborough until 1946, when he went to University College, London (UCL) as a lecturer, where he again worked under Dr. Barlow building up microwave research there. Dr. Barlow was by that time a professor at UCL.

In 1955 Alex Cullen became the first Professor of Electrical Engineering at Sheffield University, moving back in 1967 to the Pendar Chair of Electrical Engineering at UCL when Professor Barlow retired. Professor Cullen was elected to a Fellowship of the Royal Academy of Engineering and to Fellowship of the Royal Society in 1977. He holds honorary doctorates of the Universities of Hong Kong, Kent and Sheffield and in 1981 he was appointed Honorary Professor at the North Western Polytechnical University in Xian, China. Professor Cullen was appointed to the Order of the British Empire in 1960 and has been awarded the Faraday Medal of the Institution of Electrical Engineers, a Royal Medal of the Royal Society and the Microwave Career Award of the Institute of Electronics and Electrical Engineers of the USA.

In 1984 Cullen was appointed an Honorary Research Fellow in the Department of Electronic Engineering at UCL, where he still carries out research. He is also active as an industrial consultant. In 1993 he was elected an Honorary Fellow of UCL, where he spent the main part of his working life.

Alex Cullen has not lost his early interest in jazz; he has a desk at one end of his study at home, a personal computer in the middle and a set of drums at the other end!

John de DALDERBY (died 1320)

John de Dalderby is believed to have been born at Dalderby, a small village near Horncastle. The earliest recorded reference to him is as a canon of St. David's Cathedral. He was appointed archdeacon of Carmarthen in 1283 and Chancellor of Lincoln Cathedral and head of the theological school in Lincoln. On 15 January 1300 he was elected Bishop of Lincoln.

In 1301 Edward I was the guest of Bishop Dalderby at Nettleham from January to March during which time an important Parliament was held in Lincoln. Dalderby was renowned for his great learning and eloquence but he is perhaps best known for his refusal to agree to the King's request for a tax without the consent of the Pope. The Bishop instructed his archdeacons to excommunicate the King's officials if they attempted to collect the tax from ecclesiastics.

In 1308 Bishop Dalderby was required to take part in a commission appointed by the Pope to try the Knights Templar, but Dalderby tried to evade this office by pleading ill-health. He excused himself from attending a Parliament held in Lincoln in 1316 because of ill health.

Bishop John Dalderby died at Stow on 5 January 1320 and was immediately revered as a saint. Miracles were said to have taken place at his tomb in Lincoln Cathedral in 1322 and 1324. A petition was addressed to the Pope praying for his canonization but this was refused. Amongst the miracles said to have been achieved by Dalderby, the most remarkable was the restoration of speech to some inhabitants of Rutland who could only bark like dogs. Although canonization was refused, the people continued to worship at the shrine of Bishop Dalderby until it was destroyed at the Reformation.

FURTHER READING: Clubley, C. *John de Dalderby, Bishop of Lincoln 1300-1320* (1965)

Francis DASHWOOD (1708-1781)

Francis Dashwood was born in December 1708 at West Wycombe, Buckinghamshire and was the son of Sir Francis Dashwood. His early education was at Eton.

In 1745 Sir Francis Dashwood married the widow of Sir Richard Ellis and this brought him the Ellis estates in Lincolnshire and, therefore, an interest in the county. In 1732 Sir Francis founded the Society of Dilettantes and in 1741 he was elected Member of Parliament for New Romney. He was elected a Fellow of the Royal Society in 1746 and awarded the degree of Doctor of Common Law by Oxford University in 1749. He was appointed a Privy Councillor in 1761 and in the following year he was appointed Chancellor of the Exchequer. In the same year he inherited the title Baron le Despencer. He was appointed Postmaster-General in 1766.

Sir Francis made his Lincolnshire home at Nocton Hall and built a land lighthouse at Dunston to guide travellers across the Heath. This was known as Dunston Pillar and was built of limestone. It was 100 feet in height with a lantern 15 feet high at the top. The Pillar is inscribed on each side as follows :

On the South	FROM THE CITY CXXVI MILES
On the North	TO LINCOLN VI MILES
On the West	COLUMNAM HANC UTILITATI PUBLICAE
	D F DASHWOOD MDCCLI
On the East	DUNSTAN PILLAR

For many years, a light was placed in the lantern and this guided travellers across the heath but in 1808 it was damaged in a storm. By that time the heath had been enclosed and a main road existed, so the light was no longer needed.

Sir Francis was the founder of the Brotherhood of St. Francis of Wycombe, which became known as the Hellfire Club. The club met in the Golden Ball, on top of the tower of West Wycombe parish church. It is not known for certain if the Hellfire Club ever met at Dunston but it is not beyond the bounds of possibility. Sir Francis was a member of the Lincoln Literary Club which met at the Green Man Inn, about five miles from Nocton Hall.

In the 1760s, his Parliamentary duties led Sir Francis to spend most of his time in London or on his estate at West Wycombe, and it seems that he only returned to Lincolnshire on short visits. He died at West Wycombe on 11 December 1781.

FURTHER READING: Kemp, B. *Sir Francis Dashwood* (1967)

William DODD (1729-77)

William Dodd was born on 29 May 1729, the son of the Vicar of Bourne. At the age of sixteen he went up to Cambridge University and was awarded the degree of Bachelor of Arts in 1749. Dodd became devoted to a life of pleasure, earning a meagre living through writing.

In October 1753 Dodd was ordained deacon by the Bishop of Ely and was appointed curate at West Ham. For a time he carried out his duties with energy and enthusiasm and when Magdalene Hospital, London, was opened in August 1758 Dodd was invited to preach the inaugural sermon in Charlotte Street Chapel, Bloomsbury. He was awarded the chaplaincy of this charity on an honorary basis but in 1763 he was awarded a salary of a hundred guineas a year. His sermons were so popular that fashionable ladies travelled from the West End to listen and Dodd was appointed a King's Chaplain. He was also appointed tutor to one of the sons of the Earl of Chesterfield and wrote a number of books as well as being editor of the *Christian Magazine.*

Dodd then returned to Cambridge University but after the award of a Doctorate in Law he returned to London and again took up the life of a socialite. This extravagant lifestyle was partly financed by his wife who had won a prize of £1000 in a state lottery. Dodd financed the building of Charlotte Chapel in Pimlico which he named after the Queen. A fashionable and prosperous congregation attended to hear him preach in the chapel. In 1772 he became Rector of Hockliffe in Bedfordshire and Vicar of Chalgrove near Oxford.

When the living of St. George's Hanover Square became vacant in February 1774 an anonymous letter was sent to Lady Aspley offering £3,000 if a gentleman to be named later received the appointment. The letter was traced to Dodd and he was deprived of the King's Chaplaincy. So much indignation was aroused that he was forced to leave the country.

He was presented to the living of Wing in Buckinghamshire by his former pupil, now Lord Chesterfield, and returned to England after the scandal had subsided, again taking up the London social life. On 2 February 1777 Dodd preached in Magdalene Chapel and two days later forged the signature of Lord Chesterfield on a bond for £4,200. This was paid and it was not for some time that it was realised that the signature was fraudulent. Dodd managed to raise the sum due but the story had attracted considerable attention and he was committed for trial.

Dodd was found guilty at the Old Bailey and sentenced to death. Whilst in prison he worked on his last book, which he called *Prison Thoughts*. A petition against the execution contained 23,000 signatures and was over thirty-seven yards long. Although the appeal was supported by such notables as Dr. Johnson, the sentence was upheld and on Friday 27 June 1777 the execution took place. An attempt to revive him failed and he was buried at Cowley in Middlesex.

FURTHER READING: Howson, G. *The Macaroni Parson: a life of the unfortunate Dr. Dodd* (1973)

The DYMOKES of Scrivelsby

Scrivelsby Court is situated on the road from Horncastle to Revesby. The gateway is surmounted by a crowned lion, thus marking it as the home of the Sovereign's Champion. The way in which the Lord of the Manor of Scrivelsby acquired the right to this title is very interesting.

Near Falaise, where William the Conqueror was born, is a village called Fontenay-le-Marmion. The Marmion family acted as Champions to the Dukes of Normandy and when William invaded England it was Robert Marmion who accompanied him as Champion. After the Conquest Marmion was granted land which included Tamworth Castle, but the Manor of Scrivelsby was particularly assigned to him as Champion to the Sovereign. Though the descendants of Sir Robert continued to be recognised as King's Champions, there is no record before the reign of Richard II of their being called upon to carry out any special duties at a coronation. In 1292 Sir Philip, one of the last and greatest of the Marmion family, died without a male heir and in 1350 his grand-daughter married Sir John Dymock, who claimed the Championship. This was upheld and he carried out the duty at Richard II's Coronation.

At the twenty-five Coronations since, it has always been a Dymoke of Scrivelsby who has officiated and only at the Coronations of William IV and Queen Victoria was this part of the ceremony omitted. At the Coronation of Richard II in 1377 the procedure for all succeeding Coronations was laid down.

During the banquet in Westminster Hall the Champion enters clad in full armour, mounted on a white horse. The armour is selected from the Sovereign's Armoury and the horse from the Sovereign's Stable. The Champion is preceded by two knights who carry his spear and shield, with the Earl Marshal riding on his left and the Lord High Constable on his right. Three times York Herald challenges to mortal combat any person who denies the sovereign to be the rightful heir to the crown of England. Three times York Herald throws down his gauntlet which after a while is delivered to him again. The third time the Challenge is made from the top of the steps in the middle of the Hall before the Sovereign, who is then presented with a gold cup full of wine. The Sovereign then drinks to the Champion, after which the cup is delivered to him and after three bows he drinks the wine, shouting 'Long Live their Majesties' and then withdraws backwards from their presence. The cup becomes the property of the Champion.

It was said that at the Coronation of James II in 1685, a woman stepped forward and took up the gauntlet, leaving a paper to say that a Champion of rank and birth would dispute the

The Lion Gate at Scrivelsby, home of the Dymokes.

King's claim to the throne. However, no more was heard of this, and there is some doubt of the truth of the story.

During the Wars of the Roses, Sir Thomas Dymoke supported the Lancastrians and was beheaded by order of Edward IV. The King tried to atone for this act by conferring honours on the heir, Sir Robert. During the Civil War, the King's Champion, Charles Dymoke, supported the royal cause, even leaving £2,000 on his death to help the King. His successor, Edward Dymoke, was accused by the Parliamentarians of bearing 'the lewd and malicious' title of King's Champion and was fined £7,000.

The last Coronation at which the elaborate ceremonial detailed above was enacted was that of George IV and since that of Edward VII the task of the Sovereign's Champion has been to carry the Standard of England.

Matthew FLINDERS (1774-1814)

The Flinders family was of Flemish origin and first settled in Lincolnshire at the time of Vermuyden's drainage of the Fens in the previous century.

Matthew Flinders was born at Donington-in-Holland on 16 March 1774 and was educated at Cowley School in Donington and at the Grammar School in Horbling. For several generations his forebears had practised surgery and it was expected that Matthew would also enter the medical profession. It is said that he was 'induced to go to sea against the wishes of friends by reading *Robinson Crusoe'*.

Flinders entered the Navy in 1789, and in 1791 sailed under Captain Bligh on his second voyage to transport breadfruit trees from Tahiti to the West Indies. In 1794, in *Bellerophon,* he fought in the battle of the 'Glorious First of June', when Lord Howe defeated a French fleet off Brest. A shipmate of Flinders in *Bellerophon* was Henry Waterhouse, who in 1794 was given command of the *Reliance* to carry Captain Hunter to Port Jackson to become New South Wales's second Governor. Flinders wrote to Waterhouse, 'expressing a passion for exploring new countries', and in 1795 he sailed in *Reliance* under Waterhouse's command to Port Jackson. With him went his younger brother, Samuel, and the ship's surgeon, George Bass, who became his close friend.

During the ensuing years Flinders and Bass carried out a number of voyages of exploration around Port Jackson, the first two in a small boat named the *Tom Thumb*. Flinders was not with Bass when the latter discovered Bass Strait in 1797 but in 1798, in the schooner *Francis*, Flinders discovered the Kent Group of islands. and in the same year circumnavigated Tasmania, discovering the site where the capital, Hobart, now lies. During these voyages Flinders did much careful charting and recorded new and important information on the aboriginals and natural history of the area.

In 1800 Flinders returned to England to propose a complete circumnavigation of Australia, a project which received the support of Sir Joseph Banks who was President of the Royal Society. As a result in 1801 Flinders was given the command of the *Xenophon* which was renamed the *Investigator*. Although the ship was well equipped for scientific purposes, with a complement which included a botanist, an artist, a botanical draughtsman and a gardener, she was in a poor state for such a major enterprise. However, by the end of 1801 Flinders reached the south-west coast of Australia and during the next seventeen months he carried out a survey of the southern coast. In mid-1802 he sailed up the eastern coast but had to discontinue his survey through illness and the condition of the ship which was found unfit for further service.

Flinders sailed for England taking his charts and other papers in the *Porpoise* but the ship was wrecked on a coral reef. Matthew escaped and the survivors were able to build a small boat in which they returned to Port Jackson to seek help. Whilst some of the party returned to the wreck Flinders sailed in the *Cumberland* to England. War had broken out between England and France and when he put into port on the island of Mauritius Flinders was imprisoned. Whilst in captivity he started work on his navigational work *A Voyage to Terra Austral*. Flinders was released on 7 July 1810 and, on his return to England he completed his book which was published a few days before his death on 19 April 1814.

FURTHER READING: Mack, J. D. *Matthew Flinders 1774-1814* (1966)

Denis FOLLOWS (1908-1983)

Denis Follows was born in Lincoln on 13 April 1908 and was a pupil at the City School from 1919 until 1927, when he became an undergraduate at University College Nottingham. He took a prominent place in the City School from the start, both in the classroom and on the sports field. His ability as an organiser manifested itself early and he was a member of most of the school societies. He was School and House Captain, Sports Secretary and Cricket Captain. At University he was President of the Students' Union and this was followed by the Presidency of the National Union of Students. After graduating in 1932, he became Senior English Master at Chiswick Grammar School. Follows was associated with the Universities Athletics Union for more than fifty years having been elected Vice-President in 1933, Chairman in 1948 and President in 1972. After service during the war in the Royal Air Force he became Secretary for sixteen years of the British Airline Pilots' Association, for which service he was awarded an MBE in 1950.

From 1948, he was the representative of the Universities Athletics Union on the Council of the Football Association, becoming Secretary in 1962, which office he held until 1973. It was Denis Follows who was responsible for the organisation of the 1966 World Cup, for which he received a CBE. His retirement from the FA was followed by the Treasurership of the Central Council for Physical Recreation and then the Chairmanship of the British Olympic Association at the time of the controversy over British and European participation in the 1980 Moscow Olympics, which followed the Russian invasion of Afghanistan. Against much political pressure for the withdrawal of the British contingent from the Games Denis Follows stuck to the non-political ideals of the Games which went ahead as planned.

Denis Follows' organising and administrative ability together with his enthusiasm, vision, dedication and good humour earned him many honours and awards which culminated in the award of a knighthood in 1978. Sir Denis Follows died on 17 September 1983.

Charles Wilmer FOSTER (1866-1935)

Canon Foster first came to Lincolnshire in 1890 as curate at St. Andrew's Church, Grimsby. His birthplace was at Dalton near Rotherham and he was ordained deacon in 1889, serving as curate at St. Michael's Coventry. In 1893 he moved to Navenby and in 1894 to Epworth. In 1901 he was appointed to the living of Timberland, where he remained until his death in 1935.

It was Canon Foster who laid the foundations of the Lincolnshire Archives Office. He first set to work on cleaning, sorting and, where necessary, repairing the Diocesan records, moving on to the probate records and finally to the Chapter records. To carry out this work he trained several of his women parishioners at Timberland.

An important aspect of the work carried out by Canon Foster and his helpers was that of listing and indexing, as those of us who are constantly using these can appreciate. Many parish lists of incumbents were compiled for a fee of £2. 2s. 0d. In 1910, with the encouragement of Bishop King, Canon Foster founded the Lincoln Record Society which has now issued 82 volumes of the highest academic standard. These include the *Registrum Antiquissimum*, the first volumes of which were edited by Canon Foster and then jointly with Dr. Kathleen Major. After Canon Foster's death they were completed by Dr. Major.

The debt owed to Canon Foster by all who use the Lincolnshire Archives Office is difficult to assess satisfactorily in a short biography. There are so many manuscripts and books deposited in the Archives which were originally his working library that one cannot readily appreciate how difficult it would be for many of us to conduct our research had it not been for him. Indeed, because of this the Foster Library in the Lincolnshire Archives Office is probably the best of any provincial record office in the country. It has also to be remembered that all Canon Foster's academic life was carried out in addition to his parochial and diocesan duties.

James FOWLER (1828-1892)

James Fowler was born on 11 December 1828 in Lichfield. His father was a grocer and James was educated at the local Diocesan School. After leaving school he was articled to the Lichfield architect Joseph Potter, where he was trained as a lithographic artist.

In 1849, at the age of twenty, he moved to Louth to work for the County Justices on Louth Prison or House of Correction. One of his early tasks was to measure the exact height of the spire of St James's Church. Fowler went into partnership with Joseph Maugham and the firm was responsible for surveying lands at North Cotes and the planning of a sea sluice at Saltfleet Haven. In 1857 they designed replacement churches at Brinkhill and Strubby and they were the architects for the re-roofing of St. Lawrence's church, Aylesby, and for the restoration of St. Andrew's church, Fulletby. In 1856 Fowler was the architect responsible for the building of a replacement Dalby Hall.

However, Fowler's fame is as an ecclesiastical architect and in 1861 he established his own office in Louth. Later that year he married Marianne, the daughter of Rev. Samuel Sheen, rector of Stanstead, Suffolk, and they had three children. Fowler was superintending architect during the building of Grimsby Town Hall, which took place from 1861 to 1863. He received a number of commissions for the replacement of Wold churches, including Ludford (1863–65), Rigsby (1863) and Gunby St. Peters (1868-70). Under his direction, the tower and east end of St. Andrew's, Halton Holegate, were rebuilt in 1866-7 and he was responsible for the rebuilding or restoration of a large number of Lincolnshire churches. Although this was his main interest, he also worked on vicarages, banks and other buildings. These are recorded in an excellent biography by David Kaye, Sam Scorer and David Robinson, *Fowler of Louth*, which was published in 1992.

FURTHER READING: Kaye, D. Scorer, S., and Robinson, D. N., *Fowler of Louth* (1992)

John FOXE (1516-87)

John Foxe was born in Boston in 1516 and his father died soon after John's birth. He was sent to Oxford, probably as a private pupil of John Hawarden, who was a Fellow of Brasenose College. John Foxe was awarded the degree of Bachelor of Arts in 1537 and a Master's degree in 1543. He become a fellow of Magdalene College in 1539. Amongst his friends at Oxford were Hugh Latimer and William Tyndale. Foxe was an extreme Protestant and would not conform to the requirement that he attend Mass regularly and proceed to Holy Orders within seven years of election to his fellowship.

In July 1545 he resigned his fellowship. On 3 February 1547, Foxe married Agnes Randall and moved to London, where he was appointed tutor to the orphan children of Henry Howard, Earl of Surrey, who had been executed on 19 January in the same year. On the accession of Mary, in 1553 the catholic Duke of Norfolk was released from prison. Foxe was dismissed from his tutorship and he escaped to the continent.

It was at this time that the earliest draft of the work for which Foxe is best known, *Actes and Monuments*, was written. This only recorded events down to 1500 and was mainly concerned with the lives of Wycliffe and Huss. A much larger edition of the book, usually known as *The Book of Martyrs,* brought the story of the Protestant martyrs down to the end of the reign of Mary and was published in September 1559. Foxe left for England a month later and he lodged with his former pupil the Duke of Norfolk. John Foxe died in April 1587 and was buried in St. Giles's Church, Cripplegate.

FURTHER READING: Olsen, V. N. *John Foxe and the English Church* (1973)

Richard FOXE (*c*1448-1528)

Richard Foxe was born in about 1448 at Ropsley, near Grantham and he probably attended the Grammar School in Boston. His early history is uncertain but he appears to have been an undergraduate at Magdalene College, Oxford and continued his education in Paris. He is believed to have been Master of the Grammar School at Stratford-on-Avon in 1477. Foxe became Chancellor of Cambridge University and was Master of Pembroke College. The history of Richard Foxe is more certain from 1485, when he was appointed Vicar of Stepney.

After Henry VII came to the throne he conferred a number of posts on Foxe, including that of principal Secretary of State, Lord Privy Seal and, in 1487, he was appointed Bishop of Exeter. Richard Foxe baptized the future Henry VIII in 1491. In 1487, Foxe was translated to the Bishopric of Bath and Wells and in 1494 he was translated again, this time to Durham. Henry VII made him the chief commissioner for raising loans from the clergy. It is clear that the King held Foxe in high regard and he made him one of the executors of his will.

Richard Foxe was a keen educationalist and founded Corpus Christi College, Oxford, in 1515 and built and endowed a Grammar School in Taunton and the King's School, Grantham. Henry VIII, on his accession in 1509, continued to employ Foxe in all the offices which his father had conferred on him. For the last ten years of his life Foxe seems to have been totally blind and he spent most of his time on his episcopal duties in the Diocese of Durham. Bishop Foxe died on 5 October 1528 and was buried in Winchester Cathedral.

John FRANKLIN (1786-1847)

John Franklin was the twelfth son of William Franklin of Spilsby and was born on 16 April 1786. It had been intended that John should enter the church but a seaside holiday created in him a strong desire to go to sea. He was sent on a voyage by merchant ship to Lisbon in an attempt to dissuade him from this ambition without success. He entered the Royal Navy and joined the *Investigator* as a midshipman under the command of his cousin, Matthew Flinders, and sailed with him to Australia.

Franklin soon demonstrated his ability in the use of nautical and astronomical instruments and on return to England he was appointed to the *Bellerophon* in which he served at the battle of Trafalgar. After serving on a number of other ships, Franklin was appointed to command the *Trent* in January 1818 and this saw the commencement of his career as an Arctic explorer.

In 1819 he was appointed to command an expedition which was intended to explore and record the northern part of the American continent and 'to determine the latitude and longitude of the northern coast of North America...' Franklin decided to follow the line of rivers and lakes and landed at York, Manitoba, on 30 August 1819. They progressed through the Nelson and Saskatchewan Lakes, but at the Cumberland House Station he found that further progress was impossible. The party was forced to overwinter at Fort Enterprise and it was not until 14 June 1821 that they were able to start on the return journey. However, they were again overtaken by the winter and did not reach York until 14 June 1822, having covered 5,550 miles.

On return to England in October of the following year, Franklin was elected a fellow of the Royal Society. On 16 February 1825 Franklin sailed from Liverpool on another expedition, which was much better equipped for Arctic exploration, having sent in advance stores together with a party of seamen. He joined the advance party at Fort Methy on 29 June 1825 and they overwintered at Fort Franklin, proceeding westward again on 24 June 1826, eventually returning to base on 18 June 1827 and to Liverpool on 26 September 1827. The achievements of this expedition were recognised by the Geographical Society of Paris which awarded Franklin their Gold Medal. On 29 April 1829 he was knighted.

From August 1830 to December 1833, Sir John commanded the *Rainbow* in the Mediterranean and on 1836 he was appointed governor of Van Diemen's land. On 18 May 1845, Franklin again set sail for the Arctic with the specific intention of solving the problem of the North West Passage. On 26 July 1845, the *Erebus* and *Terror* entered Lancaster Sound and vanished into the unknown. Concern for their fate was not felt for some time, as the ships were provisioned for three years, but by the spring of 1848 a series of search expeditions both public and private were organised. Traces of the expedition were found, from which it was confirmed that Sir John died on 11 June 1847 and he is recognised as the discoverer of the

North West Passage. There are statues to his memory in Waterloo Place London, Hobart and Spilsby. There is also a monument in Westminster Abbey.

FURTHER READING: Beattie, O. *Frozen in time, the fate of the Franklin Expedition* (1989)

Guy GIBSON (1918-1944)

One of the most famous of Second World War holders of the Victoria Cross was Guy Gibson, who was born at Simla, India on 12 August 1918. Whilst still a baby, Guy was brought to live at Folkestone, Kent, and he attended the preparatory school there before becoming a pupil at St. Edmund's School, Oxford. After leaving school Gibson applied to Vickers Aviation for a job as a test pilot but was advised to join the Royal Air Force. This he did and was commissioned on 6 February 1937 and posted to 83 Squadron which was based at Scampton. There he flew Hawker Hind, Bristol Blenheim and Handley Page bombers after they were introduced to the Squadron on 31 October 1938.

Guy Gibson's first wartime operational flight was at 6.15 pm on the day war was declared (3 September 1939), when six Hampdens were sent to attack German Naval units but no targets were found. His second operational flight was not until 11 April 1940 but from then until September of that year he flew twenty-seven sorties and was awarded the Distinguished Flying Cross on 8 July 1940. On 13 November, Guy Gibson was posted to 29 Squadron at Digby as a Flight Lieutenant for night flying in the Bristol Beaufighter. On 29 June 1941 Gibson was promoted to Squadron Leader and awarded a bar to his DFC on 10 September. He joined 160 Squadron at Coningsby on 13 April 1942 to fly the Avro Manchester and Lancaster Bombers. Squadron Leader Gibson was awarded the Distinguished Service Order on 30 March 1943.

Having completed a tour of operations with 160 Squadron, Gibson was 'invited' by the Air Officer Commanding No. 5 Group to undertake one more special task. This was the formation of 'X' Squadron, shortly to be numbered 617 Squadron (The Dambusters). After six weeks of intense preparation nineteen Lancasters became airborne at 9.30 pm on 16 May 1943 and were led by Gibson to the primary target which was the Möhne Dam with the Sorpe dam as the secondary target. Both dams were breached but eight Lancasters failed to return. Thirty-three crew members were decorated for gallantry and Guy Gibson was awarded the Victoria Cross.

617 Squadron was stood down after the raid and Gibson was posted to the Directorate of Accidents at the Air Ministry but returned to Coningsby on 2 August 1944 in a non-operational post. However, he did manage to do some flying and on 19 September 1944, after much persuasion by him, he was allowed to take part in an attack on the railway and industrial centres at Rheydt and Mönchengladbach. After making a successful attack, on the return flight Wing Commander Gibson's Mosquito was seen to crash in flames. Together with his navigator, Guy Gibson was buried at Steenbergen, Holland.

FURTHER READING: Gibson, Guy. *Enemy Coast Ahead* (1969); Bennet, Tom. *617 Squadron* (1986)

Wing Commander Guy Gibson and his Scampton crew with 'Nigger', his dog, killed the day before the Dams raid.

GILBERT of Sempringham (*c*1085-1189)

Gilbert was born in about 1085 at Sempringham near Billingborough and was the son of Jocelin, a Norman knight, who came from Normandy with William the Conqueror. His mother was a Saxon 'of inferior origin' and was said to have dreamed before Gilbert's birth that she was holding the round moon in her lap, which was taken to be a sign that the child would rise to greatness.

Because of a deformity Gilbert was unable to follow the knightly pursuits of his father. It is believed he was shunned because of his repulsive appearance. He went to France, probably to the monastery of Citeaux, and on his return to England in 1123 his father gave him the livings of Sempringham and Torrington.

Gilbert gave the revenue of these benefices to the poor and founded and taught in free schools in his parishes. Gilbert lived in a room over the porch in the church at Sempringham and he decided to found a convent to which women could retire from the world in order to devote themselves to study and worship. The priory of Sempringham was founded in 1135 and the new Order of Gilbertines was approved by the Pope, the King and Bishop Alexander of Lincoln. Gilbertine Priories were founded at Alvingham, North Ormsby, Six Hills, West Torrington and Lincoln. Others followed until there was a total of thirteen houses for women. Men were introduced into the house to help with the heavy work but were kept strictly separate from the nuns. Although Gilbert was renowned for his gentleness, he made strict rules for discipline.

Gilbert was particularly interested in education and taught by example. He set a high example not only by his own learning and piety but also by his humility and energy. Numerous miracles were ascribed to him. In London, fire consumed the houses surrounding the one in which he was staying but he remained praying and the fire consumed all but the room in which he was situated.

In 1165 Gilbert and his Priors were summoned to Westminster, charged with assisting Thomas à Becket. Gilbert said he would suffer exile rather than say he was innocent of the charge because he believed he was right to assist the Archbishop as head of his Church. The charge was dismissed by Henry II. After his death at the supposed age of 106, the Order continued to grow and at the Dissolution there were twenty-six Gilbertine houses in England.

Gilbert was canonised in 1202 and his tomb in the Priory Church at Sempringham became a place of pilgrimage. St. Gilbert's feast day is 4 February.

FURTHER READING: Iredale, E. W. *Sempringham and Saint Gilbert and the Gilbertines* (1992); Foreville, R. *Saint Gilbert of Sempringham* (1986)

Field Flowers GOE (1831-1910)

Field Flowers Goe the younger was the son of Field Flowers Goe, an attorney of Louth. He was the grandson of Bartholomew Goe, vicar of Boston, and Frances Field, from whom the unusual first name derived. He received his early education at Louth Grammar School and in later life he used to comment on the harsh treatment the boys received at that time under a cruel and merciless master.

It was intended that Field Flowers Goe junior should follow his father's profession but at the age of twenty-one he went up to Oxford and graduated from Hertford College in 1857. Goe was ordained deacon in 1858 and appointed curate at Christ Church, Kingston-upon-Hull. He was ordained priest six months later and remained at Christ Church as perpetual curate. In 1873 he was presented to the rectory of Sunderland and in 1877 he was presented to St. George's, Bloomsbury. This fashionable parish brought his abilities as an organiser and preacher to the attention of a much wider audience and in 1884 he was appointed Select Preacher at Cambridge University.

In 1886 Field Flowers Goe became Bishop of Melbourne, Australia, succeeding Bishop Moorhouse, who had been a very eloquent and forceful person and inevitably the new Bishop was contrasted with his predecessor. The Cathedral of St. Paul, Melbourne, was still being built and he was enthroned in St. James's pro-Cathedral. He had many difficulties to overcome before the new Cathedral was consecrated in January 1891. The Diocese grew rapidly, but in 1893 a bank failure came and income fell dramatically, so any attempt to create new dioceses had to be postponed. The Bishop agreed to a cut of £500 in his salary. As the economy began to recover it was possible by 1901 to create three new dioceses which, of course, was a considerable help in easing the workload of Bishop Goe.

When his wife died in August 1901 the Bishop was so affected that he resigned in October of that year. Mrs Goe is buried at Kew and her tombstone is inscribed 'The heart of her husband did safely trust in her.' Bishop Goe after his retirement lived at first in Durham but soon moved to Wimbledon where he died on 28 June 1910.

Reginald GOODALL (1901-1990)

There is something of a mystery about the date of birth of Sir Reginald Goodall; various dates from 1902 to 1905 have been quoted. This is because he adjusted his age to suit the circumstances!

Reginald Goodall was actually born on 13 July 1901 in a terraced house, 78 Monks Road, in Lincoln. His father, Albert Edward Goodall, was a music teacher and also organist and choirmaster at St. Peter-at-Arches church. Albert's 'day job' was confidential clerk to E. E. Tweed, a Lincoln solicitor. Reginald and his brother William received their early education at Miss Wileman's private school in Nettleham Road.

Reggie was taught the piano by his half sister Agnes who lived in Tentercroft Street, where she taught music for a living. In 1910 she persuaded her father to let Reggie audition for Lincoln Cathedral choir school, where the organist and choirmaster was Dr. G. J. Bennett.

Reggie was accepted and became a boarder at the choir school, which was then at 1 Northgate. Although Bennett's methods as choirmaster were somewhat unorthodox, the choir was regarded as one of the best of its kind. Goodall always appreciated this early training which, as well as singing in the Cathedral, included lessons in piano and theory from the assistant organist.

In 1911 Albert Goodall was committed to eight month's imprisonment for forgery and after his release he emigrated to Canada, leaving behind his wife and children. Early in 1914 his wife, Adelaide, decided to join her sister in Massachusetts, taking the two boys with her. Reggie soon joined his father in Canada.

Albert Goodall was working as a piano teacher and was also organist and choirmaster at a local church. Reggie, as well as singing in the church choir, was taught piano, organ and theory at the conservatory of music in the nearby town of Hamilton. In 1916 Albert Goodall volunteered for the army and Reggie returned to his mother, working first as a railway messenger and then in an engineering works. After a few months, Reggie returned to Canada to resume his studies at Hamilton conservatory of music, paying the fees and supporting himself by working as a clerk. He was awarded a Gold Medal by Toronto University and two years later graduated with first class honours.

Goodall was appointed organist and choirmaster at Dundas and by giving piano lessons earned a meagre living. In June 1922, he was appointed organist at the church of St. Alban the Martyr, Toronto and later moved on to the nearby church of St. Mary the Virgin. In 1925 Goodall met Sir Hugh Allen, the director of the Royal College of Music in London and professor of music at Oxford University. Sir Hugh persuaded Reggie to return to London and enrol at the Royal College of Music to study piano and organ. In order to earn his keep and pay the college fees he became pianist at the King's Picture Playhouse, accompanying silent films, and he also became assistant organist at St. Alban the Martyr's church, Holborn.

He joined the conducting class at the RCM and in December 1930 conducted the first performance in Britain of Brückner's *Mass in F Minor*. Goodall left St. Alban's in June 1936, having brought the choir to a high standard. Reginald Goodall trained six of the St. Alban's choristers for the first public performance on 17 December 1934 of the young Benjamin Britten's *A Boy was Born* and this was the first of a number of occasions when he worked with Britten.

Goodall made his début as an opera conductor in April 1936 with an amateur production of *Carmen* at King George's Hall, Tottenham Court Road and later that year conducted his first professionally performed opera with the British Music Drama Company. In December 1939 he conducted the first concert of the Wessex Philharmonic Orchestra with whom he conducted regularly until his call-up in 1943.

In April 1943, he was called up for service in the Army but on 26 June he was able, whilst on leave, to conduct a concert of popular music in Swansea. On 19 September 1943 he was discharged from the army, but it was not until a year later, when he joined the Sadler's Wells Opera, that he was able to find work. On 1 November in the same year he conducted *The Barber of Seville*. On 9 March 1945 he conducted the Hallé Orchestra and this was his first introduction to Wagner. Later in his career he became regarded as the greatest conductor of Wagner of his day. Goodall conducted the premiere of Britten's *Peter Grimes* on 7 July 1945 and was appointed assistant conductor at the Royal Opera House, Covent Garden in 1946, being appointed conductor in the following year.

Reginald Goodall was now an established and popular opera conductor and in 1975 he was awarded the CBE, followed ten years later by a knighthood. He received Honorary Doctorates in Music from Oxford, Leeds and Newcastle Universities.

Sir Reginald Goodall married Eleanor Gipps, a schoolteacher, on 2 August 1932 and she died on 30 July 1978. Goodall himself died on 5 May 1990 and was buried at Barham, Kent.

FURTHER READING: Lucas, J. *Reggie. The Life of Reginald Goodall* (1993)

Barnabe GOOGE (1540-1594)

Barnabe Googe was the son of Robert Googe, the Recorder of Lincoln, and his wife, who was the daughter of Sir Walter Mantell of Alvingham.

Barnabe studied at Christ's College, Oxford but there is no record of his obtaining a degree, a not unusual circumstance at this time. On leaving Oxford he entered the service of Sir William Cecil and in 1560 he published *The first thre Bokes of the most Christian Poet, Marrcellus Palingenes called the Zodyake of Life*. This ran to several editions. In the winter of 1561 he went abroad and on his return early in 1563 his poems were published under the title *Ecloges, Epytaphs and Sonnets*. In the same year Googe was appointed one of the queen's gentlemen-pensioners and also in 1563 became engaged to Mary Danell of Scotney, Kent and they were married on 5 February 1563/4.

In 1570, a translation by Googe from the Latin of Thomas Naogenys, entitled *The Popish Kingdom or Reign of Antichrist* was published. In 1574 Googe was sent by Cecil to Ireland and in 1582 he was appointed provost marshal of Connaught. Whilst in Ireland he published in 1577 *Foure bokes of Husbandrie, collected by Conradus Heresbauchius...Newly Englished by Barnabe Googe Esquire*. Several other works were published by Googe and he returned to England in 1585. He died on 1 February 1594.

Percy GRAINGER (1882-1961)

George Percy Aldridge Grainger became well-known as a collector of folk songs, especially in Lincolnshire, but he was actually born near Melbourne, Australia in 1882.

Percy Grainger was taught to play the piano by his mother and by the age of ten began to give piano recitals to raise money to study in Frankfurt, Germany. At the age of twelve he began his studies in Germany and in 1900, together with his mother, he undertook a concert tour which brought him to England in 1901. In 1904 he appeared as a solo pianist at Grimsby and this was his first contact with Lincolnshire.

A class for folk songs was included in the North Lincolnshire Musical Competition held at Brigg in 1905 and Grainger was present. A number of folk songs were noted on this occasion which seems to have inspired Percy Grainger to start collecting seriously. Later that year he went on a 'bike tour through Lincolnshire to gather tunes', accompanied by George Elwes, the tenor, who lived at the Manor House, Brigg. Three of the songs collected at this time, *Brigg Fair*, *Seventeen come Sunday* and *March to the Battlefield*, were published in time for the 1906 folk song competition.

Grainger again visited Brigg in late July 1906 and on Saturday the 28th he went to Broughton to note three songs from Thomas Stark. He returned to Brigg where Joseph Taylor phonographed fourteen songs, George Gouldthorpe ten and George Wray seven. A similar phonographic session was held in Brigg on the following Saturday when six singers recorded 28 songs. Grainger returned to Brigg to record more songs in 1908 and in June of that year Joseph Taylor, who had contributed a considerable number of songs to Grainger's collection, travelled to London and recorded several songs for the Gramophone Company. By 4 August 1908 Grainger had compiled his manuscript collection of the songs collected in 1906 and 1908.

Percy Grainger became a concert pianist and took part in several Royal Command performances. He made many arrangements of Lincolnshire folksongs, his biggest work in that style being his *Lincolnshire Posy* for wind-band or two pianos.

Grainger died in America on 20 February 1961.

FURTHER READING: For a complete record of Grainger's work see: Sadie, S. *The New Grove Dictionary of Music and Musicians* (1980) Vol. 7. pp. 614-619.

Robert GROSSETESTE (died 1253)

Robert Grosseteste is believed to have been born in 1175 in Suffolk and was of humble origin. He appears to have studied at Oxford and in Paris and returned to Oxford as chancellor. In 1224 he became the first rector of the Franciscans at Oxford and was a skilful preacher. Grosseteste became Archdeacon of Wiltshire, Archdeacon of Northampton and prebendary of Empingham in Lincoln Cathedral.

In February 1235, following the death of Hugh de Welles, Grosseteste was elected by the chapter to the Bishopric of Lincoln. He was consecrated at Reading on 3 or 17 June 1235 and set himself the task of reforming abuses which his predecessors had left, particularly games and processions, which he believed encouraged strife, drinking bouts and the desecration of church yards.

In 1239 a quarrel arose between Grosseteste and the chapter of Lincoln Cathedral which continued for several years. The dean and canons opposed the Bishop's right to visit the chapter. The chapter instructed the incumbents of churches belonging to them to oppose the Bishop if he attempted to visit them and eventually Grosseteste was forced to suspend the dean, precentor and sub-dean. The chapter appealed to Rome but on their way met the Bishop in London and they agreed that the matter should be decided by the Bishop of Worcester and the Archdeacons of Worcester and Sudbury. This came to nothing and they returned to Lincoln. On one occasion when one of the canons was preaching against the Bishop he said 'If we were to be silent the very stones would cry out' upon which a piece of stone fell, dropping behind the dean's stall! A direct appeal was made to the Pope who, after several years' delay, in 1245 decided in favour of Grosseteste.

Robert Grosseteste was fearless in opposing both King and Pope if he thought their actions were wrong. In 1251 he opposed the appointment by the Pope of an Italian to a wealthy benefice within the diocese and in 1252 he excommunicated a Burgundian who had been appointed by the Pope to Flamstead. In the same year he opposed the King's request for a tenth of church revenues to be used to mount a crusade.

Bishop Grosseteste died on 9 October 1253 at Buckden and was buried in Lincoln Cathedral. Miracles were soon reported and it was said that 'the melodious sound of a great bell was heard coming from the sky but there was no convent near'. It was also said that Franciscan Friars who were travelling to Buckden heard the sound of bells. The regard with which the Bishop was held led to several requests to the Pope for his canonization but these were unsuccessful.

FURTHER READING: Srawley, J. H. *Robert Grosseteste, Bishop of Lincoln* (1966)

John GRUNDY Snr. (1696-1748)

John Grundy Snr. was born in Leicestershire in 1696 and although he appears to have only received a rudimentary education he became a surveyor and a teacher of mathematics. The first surveying task which Grundy undertook appears to have been the estate of a Mr. Jennens of Gopsall Park near Congerstone, in which he suggested a scheme for an improved water supply to the house. In 1729 he made a survey of Atterton in South Leicestershire.

Two years later he went to Spalding to survey the Lincolnshire estates of the Duke of Buccleuch which involved the study of drains, outfalls, banks and sluices. It also involved the study of the relationship of the height of the land to sea level. Grundy considered the drainage of the flat fenlands and applied his mathematical knowledge to bringing 'drainage to an art strictly mathematical and philosophical'.

Spalding now became the centre of Grundy's activities and on 1 March 1732 he presented a paper entitled *Propositions for Draining of the Parishes and Deeping Great Fenn in the Wapentake of Elloe in the parts of South Holland in Lincolnshire* to the Spalding Gentlemen's Society. This seems to have created considerable interest and in 1733 Grundy was employed by the Commissioners of Sewers to make a survey of the parish of Moulton. In the following year he became involved with the drainage of Deeping Fen, which was his main preoccupation for the remainder of his life. In 1735 Grundy completed his treatise on *The Art of Drainage*.

He made a report on the drainage of Moulton Salt Marsh in 1739 and prepared a scheme for the repair of the sea defences at Happisburgh in Norfolk in 1742. In 1744 he produced an important report on the improvement of the River Witham. John Grundy Snr. died aged 52 and is buried at Congerstone. His son John, Jnr. erected an altar tomb which bears the inscription: 'In memory of John Grundy late of Spalding in Lincolnshire, who without the advantage of a liberal education, had gained by his industry a competent knowledge in several of the learned sciences and by all ingenious honest men deservedly beloved and died by all such truly regretted.'

John GRUNDY Jnr. (1719-1783)

John Grundy Jnr. was born at Market Bosworth Leicestershire and baptized at Congerstone on 1 July 1719. He moved with his parents to Spalding on 27 December 1739 and it was from his father that he learned mathematics and other theoretical and practical skills upon which his own career was to be founded. As well as having the scientific and mathematical knowledge which his father considered essential, John Grundy Jnr. had an artistic flair which was expressed in his draughtsmanship and the decorative details of his plans and in the title pages of his *Book Maps*.

The first project which John Grundy Jnr. undertook on his own account appears to have been the construction in 1739 of a sluice in Pinchbeck, where the Blue Gowt Drain entered the River Glen. Two years later he published his first report as an engineering consultant in which he objected to a scheme to divert the course of the Trent Navigation. From 1745 he was employed by the Duke of Ancaster on a number of schemes to improve the grounds at Grimsthorpe Castle and to bring running water to the house.

In 1748 John Grundy Jnr. was appointed agent and surveyor to the Adventurers of Deeping Fen and assumed charge of the continuous programme of repairs and improvements. Grundy experimented with the use of various materials on the banks of the drains in order to assess their effectiveness in resisting erosion. The main river in Lincolnshire is, of course, the Witham, which, from Lincoln, is connected to the Trent by the Roman Fossedyke. In 1740 Richard Ellison restored the Fossedyke and this created interest in the improvement of that part of the Witham which connected Lincoln with Boston.

In 1743 the Grundys, father and son, made a detailed survey of the Witham and in the following year published a report with three alternative schemes for improving the river. Nothing was done but discussions took place periodically until 1764 when work started on the Great Sluice in Boston. In 1756 Grundy Jnr. produced a scheme for a canal from Louth to Tetney, but it was not until 13 February 1765 that sufficient money was available for work to commence. The canal was completed under Grundy's supervision in May 1770.

From 1760 until 1776 John Grundy, Jnr., often in partnership with John Smeeton, produced a considerable number of reports and supervised schemes both in Lincolnshire and further afield. After about 1772 he only accepted work in the vicinity of Spalding and by about 1776 he appears to have retired altogether. Grundy Jnr. was a founder member of the Society of Civil Engineers, which was founded by John Smeeton in 1771. He died in Spalding on 15 June 1783 and is buried in the parish church.

FURTHER READING: Wright, N. R. *John Grundy of Spalding, Engineer 1719-1783* (Lincoln 1983)

John George HAIGH (1909-1949)

In 1949 Haigh became known as 'The Acid Bath Murderer' because of the way in which he disposed of his victims.

He was born in Stamford and his parents were very strict Plymouth Brethren. His father, who was an electrician, became unemployed about three months before John was born. Young Haigh was not allowed to play with other children but his parents bought him a puppy and pet rabbits. Eventually the family moved to Wakefield and John's lifestyle changed abruptly. From the very strict puritanical regime of the Plymouth Brethren he became involved with the High Church Anglican Cathedral. Haigh became a member of the choir and a server, spending all day on Sundays in the Cathedral. He won a scholarship to the Grammar School and whilst still at school he was appointed assistant organist at the Cathedral.

His first prison sentence was for fraudulent hire-purchase deals and selling non-existent cars. He was released in December 1935 and decided to set up a dry-cleaning business in London. However, in fact he became a chauffeur/secretary to the McSwan family, who were later to become his victims, but after a short time he decided to become a solicitor without bothering to qualify! Not surprisingly, he was soon arrested for fraud and sentenced to four years imprisonment. In June 1941 he was again arrested, this time for theft, and sentenced to twenty-one months imprisonment. This sentence was served in Lincoln Prison and it was here that his thoughts turned to murder.

Haigh worked in the tinsmith's workshop where sulphuric acid was readily available. Prisoners who worked in the fields outside the prison brought him fieldmice upon which he was able to practise disposing of the bodies in the acid.

Several years after his release and return to London he became friendly with Olive Durand-Deacon, a wealthy widow, whom he shot in February 1949 and disposed of her body in a forty-gallon drum, which he filled with sulphuric acid. He was eventually arrested and tried at Lewes Assizes on 18 and 19 July 1949. Haigh confessed to eight other murders and despite a plea of insanity he was found guilty and executed on 10 August 1949.

FURTHER READING: *The Times* 19 & 20 July 1949, *Lincolnshire Echo* 18 & 19 July 1949, *Lincolnshire Chronicle* 23 July 1949; La Bern, A. *Haigh: The Mind of a Murderer* (1973)

John HARRISON (1693-1776)

John Harrison was born at Foulby in the parish of Wragby, Yorkshire, in March 1693 and was the eldest son of Henry Harrison. His father was a carpenter and joiner to Sir Roland Winn of Nostell Priory. Henry Harrison also turned his hand to the repair of clocks. When John was seven years old the family moved to Barrow-on-Humber, where Sir Roland Winn had an estate.

Young John received little education but developed an interest in machinery. He often helped his father in his workshop and in 1715 John constructed an eight-day clock made entirely of wood, which is now in the Science Museum. To offset the effect of heat and cold on timekeeping John devised in 1720 the 'grid iron pendulum'. He went on to make other improvements in clockmaking.

In 1713 an Act was passed offering rewards of £10,000, £15,000 and £20,000 to anyone who could devise a method of detecting longitude at sea within sixty, forty and thirty miles respectively. Harrison went to London in 1728 with drawings and he was advised to construct his chronometer for examination by the Board of Longitude. In 1736 Harrison tested his chronometer on a voyage to Lisbon and £500 was paid to him. A second chronometer was made in 1739 and a third received the Coply Award in 1749. A fourth chronometer, made in the form of a pocketwatch five inches in diameter, was finished in 1759.

This went on trial on a voyage to Jamaica from 18 November 1761 to 26 March 1762 and Harrison was paid £5000. Further tests were made and the sum paid to him was made up to half that to which he was entitled. It was not until the King intervened that he was paid the remainder on 14 June 1773.

Harrison died three years later on 24 March 1776 at Hampstead.

FURTHER READING: Knight, F. *John Harrison, the man who made navigation safe* (1962)

Thomas HEYWOOD (*c*1574-1641)

In a funeral eulogy for Sir George St. Poole, the playwright, Thomas Heywood refers to him as his 'countryman'. Although it would appear that Heywood was born in Lincolnshire in about 1574 it is uncertain exactly where his birthplace was. He became an actor on the London stage, and a member of the Queen's company in 1619. Heywood's plays include *The Four Prentices of London*, *Edward IV* in two parts and *A Woman Killed with Kindness*. Altogether he wrote or collaborated in the writing of about 220 plays. He wrote a number of poems and rhyming translations from Lucius, Erasmus and Ovid.

FURTHER READING: Baines, B. J. *Thomas Heywood* (1984)

Francis HILL (1899-1980)

James William Francis Hill was born on 15 September 1899 and was the son of a draper. He was baptised into the Newland Congregational Church and attended the Municipal Technical School (later the City School) in Lincoln. Francis Hill went up to Trinity College, Cambridge but his studies were interrupted when he was commissioned in the King's Royal Rifle Corps during the first World War. After brief service in France he returned to Cambridge and after graduating in Law he returned to Lincoln, joining a firm of solicitors (now Andrew & Co.).

The friendship of Canon C. W. Foster, the founder of the Lincoln Record Society, and other academics encouraged Francis Hill to submit papers for publication by several local societies and between 1948 and 1974 Cambridge University Press published his four volume history of Lincoln: *Medieval Lincoln, Tudor and Stuart Lincoln, Georgian Lincoln*, and *Victorian Lincoln*. The Lincoln Civic Trust published Hill's *A Short History of Lincoln* and the Lincoln Record Society published *The Letters and Papers of the Banks Family of Revesby Abbey 1704-1760*.

It was not only historical research that occupied Francis Hill's spare time. He was Chancellor of Nottingham University from 1972 to 1978, treasurer of the Lincoln Diocesan Record Office from 1935 and vice-chairman of the Lincolnshire Archives Committee. The provision of an archive service for the whole of the county was one of his interests. In *Lincolnshire History and Archaeology* Vol. 13, 1978 he recorded the process by which the city and three administrative parts of the county together with the muniments of the Bishop and dean and chapter were brought together. Francis Hill deposited much of his own collection of historical documents in the new archives and encouraged others to do the same.

Francis Hill served on Lincoln City Council as a Councillor, Alderman and Mayor. He was chairman of the Association of Municipal Corporations from 1957 to 1966 and represented that body on the council of the British Records Association from 1947 until 1973. From 1967 until 1971 he was president of the International Union of Local Authorities. His service to local government was recognised when a knighthood was conferred on him in 1958. Hill had

Sir Francis Hill

remarkable powers of concentration which enabled him to achieve so much but his manner and persuasiveness helped him enlist assistance from others. He died suddenly on 6 January 1980.

FURTHER READING: Hill, Sir Francis *Medieval Lincoln* (Reprint 1990) pp. 1-12

William HILTON (1786-1839)

William Hilton was born on 3 June 1786 in Lincoln. His father was a portrait painter and William was apprenticed to J. R. Smith, an engraver. Peter de Wint was also with Smith at the same time.

Hilton's earliest known works are designs in oil for *The Mirror* and *The Citizen of the World*. He commenced to exhibit at the Royal Academy in 1803. In 1810 Hilton was awarded a premium by the British Institution and in the following year he received a further premium for his picture of *The Entombment of Christ*. The Institution also bought his *Mary anointing the feet of Jesus* which had been exhibited at the Royal Academy in 1813, and *Christ crowned with Thorns* which had been exhibited in 1825.

In 1813 he was elected an associate and in 1818 a full member of the Royal Academy. In 1827 he became keeper of the Academy and in 1828 he married the sister of his friend Peter de Wint. It is said that William Hilton's health was ruined by the death of his wife in 1835 and he died on 30 December 1839.

Michael HONYWOOD (1597-1681)

Michael Honywood was born in 1597 and was the sixth son of Robert and Elizabeth Honywood of Charing in Kent and Marks Hall in Essex. He graduated with the degree of Bachelor of Arts at Christ's College, Cambridge in 1614 and received his Master's Degree in 1618. In 1636 he was awarded the degree of Bachelor of Divinity. Honywood was elected to a fellowship at Christ's College and became Proctor in 1628. He was awarded a Doctorate in Divinity in 1660.

In 1640 Michael Honywood was appointed to the living of Kegworth in Leicestershire but appears to have been non-resident. In 1642 he went to the Low Countries, residing at Utrecht, where he remained during the Protectorate. A new rector was appointed to Kegworth in 1649. At the Restoration Honywood returned to England and resumed the living of Kegworth.

On 12 October 1660 he was installed as Dean of Lincoln Cathedral and he immediately set to work to repair the damage to the Cathedral which had been done during the Interregnum. He re-established choral services, but the work for which Honywood is best remembered is the building of what has become known as the Wren Library. This was carried out at a cost of £780, which Honywood paid himself. The work was to the design of Sir Christopher Wren and Honywood gave his collection of books to the Chapter for housing in the new library. These include rare seventeenth century tracts but some books printed by Caxton and Wynkyn de Worde were later sold.

Dean Michael Honywood died on 7 September 1681 at the age of 85.

FURTHER READING: Srawley, J. H. *Michael Honywood, Dean of Lincoln 1660-81* (1950)

HUGH of Avalon (?1135-1200)

St. Hugh, Bishop of Lincoln, was born at Avalon in Burgundy in about 1135. Hugh was a Carthusian monk and when Henry II founded a monastery of that Order at Witham in Somerset he sent for him to take charge of it. Hugh refused to go to Witham until Henry agreed to find accommodation and to compensate those who had been turned out of their homes to make room for the monastery.

This was typical of Hugh's attitude to the rather overbearing King — good temper and firmness. He was able to soothe the King with a joke, often at the King's expense. He calmed the rage of Richard I with a kiss and yet still refused to pay taxes to finance the King's war in France.

In 1186 Hugh became Bishop of Lincoln, which was the largest diocese in England. He was faced with rebuilding the cathedral which had been severely damaged by an earthquake and also had to reorganise the administration of the diocese which had, for almost twenty years, been without a resident Bishop. Following the death of Robert Chesney in 1166 there had been a vacancy until Geoffrey, the King's illegitimate son, was appointed in 1173. He spent little time in the diocese and resigned in 1182. Walter of Coustances was elected Bishop

Late 15th. century portrait of St. Hugh, by the Master of Amiens.

in 1183 but was transferred to Rouen in the following year and there was a vacancy until Hugh's appointment.

Hugh was easily aroused to anger, particularly when he found injustice in any form and he stood up alone before rioting mobs incensed against the Jews. Although Hugh was no respecter of persons he himself was regarded highly and when he died at Lincoln's Inn in London on 16 November 1200 the coffin was met on the outskirts of Lincoln by the Kings of England and Scotland, three archbishops, numerous bishops, abbots and nobles. King John was one of those who helped carry the coffin to its resting place in Hugh's Cathedral. Hugh was canonised in 1220.

FURTHER READING: Farmer, D. H. *Saint Hugh of Lincoln* (1985)

Little St. HUGH (died 1255)

In 1255 the body of a nine year old boy was found in a well in the house now known as Jews' Court on Steep Hill in Lincoln. The house is believed to have contained the Jewish Synagogue and it was alleged that Hugh was the victim of ritual murder. A large number of Jews were tortured and hanged but, as with a number of other such cases, no actual proof was forthcoming that the murder was carried out by the Jews.

The story is retold by the Prioress in Chaucer's *Canterbury Tales* and also in a lengthy poem published by Sir Walter Scott in 1802 in *A Minstrelsy of the Scottish Border*. In the early years of this century 'St. Hugh's Well' could be seen in the basement of Jews' Court but, when in 1928 the City Council decided to demolish the house, they agreed to preserve the well. However, it was discovered that, because no trace of the original well could be found, the previous owner had a mock well made in a dark corner of the basement. This was filled with water and sometimes the water overflowed and trickled down the street! Fortunately Jews' Court was preserved and is now the headquarters of the Society for Lincolnshire History and Archaeology.

John HUNT (1812-1848)

John Hunt was born at Hykeham Moor near Lincoln on 13 June 1812 but the family moved to Balderton near Newark and there he spent his boyhood.

Young John commenced his working life as a ploughboy at the age of ten. His father had been a soldier and, as a result of the stories that he told him, John decided that he too wanted an adventurous life and decided to join the army. His parents were God-fearing and taught their children the elements of religion. At the age of fifteen John was taken ill with rheumatic fever and during his slow recovery he studied the Bible and was persuaded to join the Methodist Church. Whilst working at Swinderby he came under the influence of John Smith who was an enthusiastic revivalist and it was at Thorpe on the Hill that John Hunt was converted.

His employer made available to John his extensive library and also encouraged him to preach at the local chapel. In due course he became a popular preacher on the Lincoln Circuit and was recommended for the Ministry. In 1835 John Hunt was proposed for service overseas and he was sent to the Theological Institution at Hoxton. It was the formidable Mrs Brackenbury of Raithby Hall who offered to bear the expense of sending Hunt to Fiji.

On 6 March 1838 he married Hannah Summers at Newton on Trent and, with other missionaries, they sailed for Fiji on 29 April. John studied carefully the religious beliefs and customs of the Fijian Islanders and decided on a policy which incorporated some of their ideas into Christian worship. The Christian Church gradually grew amongst the Fijians and John learned the language so that he could preach to the Islanders in the native tongue. He translated the New Testament into Fijian and he became greatly respected amongst the islanders. Unfortunately the strain of the mission field took its toll and he died on 4 December 1848 at the age of 36.

The Minutes of the Methodist Conference of 1849 recorded his death as follows : 'Mr Hunt was a man of intellectual energy and of a piety which breathed the purest spirit of love to God and charity to man' In 1909 the chapel at Thorpe-on-the Hill where John Hunt was converted was rebuilt and named The John Hunt Memorial Chapel.

FURTHER READING: Rowe, G. S. *The Life of John Hunt* (1855); Birtwhistle, A. *In His Armour* (1954).

Annie HUTCHINSON (?1590-1643)

Annie Hutchinson was born in 1590 or 1591 and was the daughter of Francis Marbury, the master of Alford Grammar School and a priest. Around 1612 she married William Hutchinson of Alford. Their eldest son Edward, in 1633, accompanied the Rev. John Cotton to Massachusetts and in September of the following year Annie and William joined him.

Annie Hutchinson was an enthusiastic admirer of Cotton's preaching and held meetings twice a week for women in support of Cotton's ministry. Eventually a difference arose between Cotton and Mrs Hutchinson and a synod at Boston on 30 August 1637 condemned her doctrines. In November she was tried and sentenced to banishment and in 1638 settled with her husband on Rhode Island.

In 1642 William Hutchinson died and Annie moved to New York County, but soon afterwards, she was murdered by Indians together with her servants and all but one of her children - a total of sixteen people. Her surviving son Edward was also murdered by Indians in 1675.

FURTHER READING: Battis, E. *Saints and Sectories: Annie Hutchinson and the Antinomian Controversy in the Massachusetts Bay Colony* (1962)

Jean INGELOW (1829-1897)

The Ingelows owned a bank, which collapsed in 1825, in Boston. The family moved to Ipswich after the bankruptcy but not before Jean was born in Boston on 17 March 1829. She was the first child of William and Jean Ingelow. They eventually had four daughters and four sons. The sons were taught by a local clergyman and the daughters by their mother.

Jean began writing verse and contributed to the *Youths' Magazine* and later became the editor. Although Jean never married, her early poems contain many references to an unhappy love affair. The family settled well in Suffolk, but they kept in touch with their cousins the Pyes, who lived in Louth. When the bank in Ipswich, for which Jean's father worked, also collapsed, the Ingelows moved again, this time to London. Jean was persuaded to publish a collection of poems and as a result *A Rhyming Chronicle of Incidents and Feelings* was published in 1850. She wrote many poems and short stories, but it was not until 1863 that her second book, *Poems,* was published. This brought the comment from Alfred Tennyson 'Miss Ingelow, I do declare you do the trick better than I do'. The book went to no fewer than thirty editions.

When Tennyson died in 1892, a petition was sent to Queen Victoria asking that Jean Ingelow be appointed poet laureate in his place, but presumably the Queen did not favour a female poet. Jean Ingelow's most famous poem, *High Tide on the Coast of Lincolnshire 1571*, is still included in present-day anthologies.

Jean died on 20 July 1897 and a memorial window was placed in St. Botolph's Church, Boston.

FURTHER READING: Peters, M. *Jean Ingelow, Victorian Poetess* (1972)

Herbert INGRAM (1811-1860)

Herbert Ingram was born on 27 May 1811 at Boston and educated at Loughton's Charity School and the Public School in Wormgate. At the age of fourteen he was apprenticed to Joseph Clarke, a local printer. From 1832 to 1834 he worked as a journeyman printer in London and in about 1834 settled in Nottingham as a printer, bookseller and newsagent, in partnership with his brother-in-law Nathaniel Cooke. The business prospered and the partners looked around for other business propositions.

They came upon a descendant of one Thomas Parr who was said to have lived to the age of 152 and claimed that his longevity was due to a vegetable pill. The secret recipe was purchased by Ingram and the resulting pills were sold with a pamphlet entitled *The Life and Times of Old Parr who lived to be 152.*

In 1842, Ingram and his partner moved to London and on 14 May in the same year they launched the first number of the *Illustrated London News.* This was intended to be an illustrated weekly record of crime but they were persuaded to make it more general in character. The first number, which was priced at 6d., contained sixteen pages of text and thirty-two

wood cuts. The best artists and writers of the day were employed and the circulation soon reached 66,000. The issue containing the report of the funeral of the Duke of Wellington in 1852 sold 250,000 copies.

At Christmas 1855 coloured prints were used for the first time. Rival illustrated magazines appeared, but all were short-lived and sold out to Ingram. The partners produced several other magazines and also turned to book publishing.

From 7 March 1856 Ingram was Member of Parliament for Boston and in 1859 he left England with his eldest son, partly for health reasons and partly to obtain illustrations for a report of the Prince of Wales's tour of America. In 1860 he toured Canada but on 7 September, whilst sailing in a paddle steamer on an excursion on Lakes Michigan and Superior, the ship collided with another and sank immediately, drowning most of the passengers including Ingram and his son.

Ingram was buried at Boston and two years later a statue to his memory was erected close to St. Botolph's Church.

Leonard James KEYWORTH (1893-1915)

Leonard Keyworth was born on 12 August 1893 and was the son of James Keyworth, a tailor, who lived at 22 Coningsby Street, Lincoln. He was educated at Rosemary Lane Wesleyan School and the Municipal Technical School (now the City School).

When Leonard left school he was employed for a short time in his father's tailoring business before entering the offices of the Lincoln engineering firm, William Foster & Co. He later joined the clerical staff of Burton, Scorer and White, solicitors. Leonard Keyworth was a member of the choir of the United Methodist Church in Silver Street and was a keen sportsman. He played cricket for the Rechabites and YMCA clubs.

Keyworth enlisted as a private in the 24th Battalion of the London Regiment on 16 September 1914 and was posted to France in early 1915. Not long after his arrival in France he took part in the action for which he was awarded the Victoria Cross. The citation published in the *London Gazette* for 3 July 1915 reads as follows: 'For most conspicuous bravery at Givenchy on the night of 25/26 May 1915. After the successful assault on the German position by the 24th Battalion London Regiment efforts were made by that unit to follow up their success by a bomb-attack, during the progress of which fifty-eight men of a total of seventy-five became casualties. During this very fierce encounter Lance-Corporal Keyworth stood fully exposed for two hours on the top of the enemy's parapet and threw about 150 bombs amongst the Germans who were only a few yards away'.

The investiture by King George V took place at Buckingham Palace on 12 July 1915 and his sister, Lily, travelled from Lincoln to be present. On his return to Lincoln a number of receptions and other ceremonies took place but Leonard Keyworth was anxious to return to France to be with his comrades. Tragically, he was killed by gunshot wounds to the head on 19 October 1915 and is buried in Abbeville Cemetery, France. The London County Council founded a memorial fund to provide book prizes for schoolchildren and each book contained a note on which was inscribed: 'LONDON COUNTY COUNCIL - KEYWORTH V C MEMORIAL PRIZE.'

I am indebted to Mr B. Martin for permission to quote from his unpublished paper *Victoria Cross Awards to members of the Lincolnshire Regiment,* a copy of which is deposited in the Local Studies Room of Lincoln Central Library. Unfortunately space does not permit a full account of other 'Yellow Bellies' who have been awarded the Victoria Cross. However, brief details will be found in *The Register of the Victoria Cross* (revised and enlarged edition 1988) published by *This England* and Mr Martin's paper mentioned above gives full details of those who served in the Lincolnshire Regiment. The following is a list of all those recipients born in the county. The rank given is that at the time the VC was awarded.

CLIFFORD, Lt. The Hon. Henry Hugh, Rifle Brigade. Born at Irnham on 15 September 1826, Gazetted 24 February 1857.

CUNNINGHAM, Cpl. John, East Yorkshire Regiment. Born at Scunthorpe 28 June 1897, Gazetted 13 June 1917.

HOBSON, Sgt. Frederick, First Central Ontario Regiment. Born at Brigg 23 November 1875, Gazetted 17 October 1917.

JACKSON, Sgt. Harold, East Yorkshire Regiment. Born Kirton-in-Holland 2 June 1892, Gazetted 8 May 1918.

NEEDHAM, Private Samuel, Bedfordshire Regiment. Born at Great Limber 16 August 1885, Gazetted 30 October 1918.

SHARPE, Cpl. Charles Richard. 2nd Battalion Lincolnshire Regiment. Born at Pickworth 29 June 1915, Gazetted 29 June 1915.

UPTON, Cpl. James. 1st Battalion Sherwood Foresters. Born in Lincoln 3 May 1888, Gazetted 29 June 1915.

See also Bromhead, Gonville (page 19)

Edward KING (1829-1910)

Edward King was born in 1829 and in 1885 became the sixtieth Bishop of Lincoln. He was a scholar and high churchman but is best remembered as a lover of people no matter what their station in life. King began his ministry as an assistant curate at Wheatley, Oxfordshire. The nearby Theological College at Cuddesdon had recently opened and King became its Chaplain and later Principal and Vicar of Cuddesdon. He was also awarded a Professorship in Pastoral Theology in the University of Oxford. In January 1885 Edward King was asked to become Bishop of Lincoln in succession to Bishop Wordsworth. The new Bishop had said that he wanted to be the Bishop of the poor and he soon took over the onerous task of preparing prisoners in Lincoln Prison for execution.

He said that his happiest times were when confirming in country parishes and it was Bishop King who transferred the official residence of the Bishops from Riseholme to Lincoln so that he was more accessible to the clergy. King was a great advocate of Retreats and Quiet Days for clergy and laity alike and he came to be recognised as a true man of God. Many believed they had a Saint amongst them. Unfortunately he had enemies and King's name will always be remembered in connection with his trial in 1890 before Archbishop Benson's court.

On 4 December 1887 Bishop King celebrated Holy Communion at St. Peter at Gowt's Church, Lincoln. It was customary in that church to have lighted candles on the altar and the Bishop faced eastwards away from the congregation. At the Offertory he mixed water with the wine. At the absolution and the concluding blessing the Bishop faced the congregation and made the sign of the cross with upraised hand. Among the congregation was one

Ernest de Lacy Read, a solicitor and churchwarden from Cleethorpes. With two parishioners, Read petitioned the Archbishop of Canterbury asking that Bishop King be brought to trial for ritual offences, the mixing of water with the wine, the use of the eastward position, the singing of the *Agnus Dei*, the use of candles when not needed for the giving of light, and the making of the sign of the cross at the absolution and benediction.

The trial began on 4 February 1890 before the Archbishop of Canterbury and five Bishops. The proceedings lasted for three weeks, after which the Archbishop reserved judgment. After much consultation the judgement was delivered on 21 November 1890 and was in favour of the Bishop with the exception of the mixing of the water and wine during the service, and it was ordered that the use of the sign of the cross at the absolution and benediction should be discontinued. Although the eastward position might be used, care should be taken that the 'manual acts' of consecration should be witnessed by the congregation.

The result of the trial was to strengthen the affection in which Edward King was held and to mark his eightieth birthday money was subscribed to build a new church in Grimsby. Early in 1910 his health began to decline and shortly after taking the Sacrament Bishop King died on 8 March 1910.

FURTHER READING: Newton, J. A. *Search for a Saint : Edward King* (1977); Chadwick, W. O. *Edward King, Bishop of Lincoln 1885-1910* (1968)

Daniel LAMBERT (1770-1809)

Valentines Series

One of the largest men for whom authentic records exist was born on 13 March 1770 in the parish of St. Margaret's Leicester. He was the eldest of the two sons of Daniel Lambert, who was huntsman to the Earl of Stamford and became keeper of Leicester Gaol. Daniel junior succeeded his father to this post in 1791.

In his youth Daniel Lambert had been a very enthusiastic participant in field sports and a keen walker and swimmer but, although he only drank water, in 1793 his weight was 32 stones. Because of his increasing weight in 1805 he resigned from the prison service and began to profit from his corpulence. A special carriage was made for him and in 1806 he commenced 'receiving company' at No. 5 Piccadilly, London. He travelled to Cambridge and then to Huntingdon and Stamford where he died at the Waggon and Horses Inn on 21 July 1809. His

EVERY VISITOR TO STAMFORD
SHOULD CALL AT
THE "LONDON" INN,
ST. JOHN'S STREET,

And see the wonderful Clothing of the celebrated Human Mammoth.

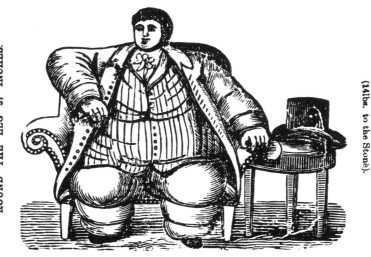

ROUND THE BODY 112 INCHES.
ROUND THE LEG 37 INCHES.

WEIGHING 52 STONES 11 POUNDS
(14lbs. to the Stone).

DANIEL LAMBERT

Who died and was buried at Stamford in June, 1809.

Also the **MINIATURE CLOTHING** presented by the Original

GENERAL TOM THUMB,

When only 15lbs. in weight,

To be shown with the above as the greatest contrast ever witnessed.

Photographs of Lambert and his Gravestone 6d. each. History of his Life, 3d. each

---

Wines, Spirits, Ales, Stout, Cigars, &c.

YE "OLD LONDON" TAVERN,
St. John's Street, Stamford.

T. T. WELLS, Proprietor.

coffin was built on two axle-trees and four wheels and it was rolled down a gradual slope from the Inn to the cemetery of St. Martin's Church, Stamford Baron. At the time of his death Daniel Lambert was 5ft. 11 inches tall and weighed 53 stone.

Bennet LANGTON (1737-1801)

Bennet Langton was born at Langton near Spilsby and was a member of the ancient Langton family, which has lived there for many centuries. The earliest known member of the family is Robert de Langton who died c1160 and the line has only recently died out.

Whilst still a young man he was introduced to Dr. Samuel Johnson who at once took a liking to him. Bennet Langton went up to Trinity College, Oxford and was visited there by Johnson in 1760. 'The Great Cham of Literature', as Johnson was known, visited Bennet's Lincolnshire home in 1764, which brought the family to the notice of 'society'. There are a number of incidents relating to this friendship but perhaps the most famous took place on the occasion of this visit when Johnson decided to roll down a steep hill at the back of the house which is known as the Sheepwalks. The Langtons, considering that the great man was rather corpulent and in his mid fifties, tried to persuade Johnson not to attempt this dangerous exercise. But Johnson was not to be put off!

On 24 May 1770 Bennet Langton married Mary, the widow of the Earl of Rothes. Langton was a founder member of the Literary Club and became a captain in the Lincolnshire Militia. Johnson visited his friend in camp in 1778 and 1783. Langton attended Dr. Johnson in his last illness and was left a book and a sum of £750 from which to pay an annuity to Johnson's black servant.

Stephen LANGTON (c1160-1228)

Archbishop Stephen Langton was the son of Henry Langton and was certainly a native of Lincolnshire. Professor Powicke has left little doubt that his birthplace was Langton near Wragby.

Little is known of his early life but he may have received his early education at the nearby Gilbertine priory at Bullington. It is known that he and his brother Simon studied art and theology at the University of Paris. Stephen remained for more than twenty years in Paris and was presented to a prebend in the Cathedral. He acquired a reputation for learning and holiness. In 1206 Stephen Langton was called to Rome by the Pope as cardinal-priest of the church of St. Chrysogonus. As the most illustrious living churchman of English birth, in 1207 he was elected Archbishop of Canterbury against the wishes of King John. He was banned from his archbishopric and it was not until 1213 that Archbishop Langton was able to return to England.

Stephen Langton led an assembly of barons and others who were dissatisfied with the rule of King John which met at St. Albans in 1213. Their grievances were discussed and

Langton read to the assembly the charter of liberties of Henry I and it was agreed that a similar charter should be imposed on King John. Archbishop Langton played a considerable role in the drafting of the Magna Carta, which was sealed by King John in 1215. Unfortunately the King soon renounced the charter and suspended the Archbishop but John died just over a year after the sealing of Magna Carta.

Archbishop Langton was able to live peacefully for the remainder of his life and he, together with the abbot of Fountains, made the investigations which resulted in the canonization of Bishop Hugh of Lincoln in 1220. When Stephen Langton died in 1228 an attempt was made for his canonization but this was never granted.

FURTHER READING: Powicke, F. M. *Stephen Langton* (1965)

Robert G. LATHAM (1812-88)

Robert Latham was born at Billingborough on 24 March 1812 and was the eldest son of the Vicar, Thomas Latham. He was educated at Eton College and in 1829 he went up to King's College, Cambridge, where he graduated Bachelor of Arts in 1832. Latham studied philology at several places on the continent and in 1839 he was elected professor of the English language and literature at University College, London. He produced a text book on *The English Language* in 1841 but in the following year turned to medicine and became a licentiate of the Royal College of Physicians.

After obtaining the degree of Doctor of Medicine in the University of London, he returned to his first love and in 1852 he became director of the etymological department of Crystal Palace. Latham undertook a thorough revision of Dr. Samuel Johnson's *Dictionary of the English Language* which he completed in 1870. Robert Latham published twenty-four other works. His books on the English language passed through many editions and for some years were regarded as authoritative. He died at Putney on 8 March 1888.

David Herbert LAWRENCE (1885-1930)

D. H. Lawrence was born at Eastwood, Nottinghamshire and was the son of a collier. He made his first visit to Lincolnshire in 1901 when he stayed with his aunt at Skegness to convalesce from pneumonia. In 1906 he stayed with his family at Mablethorpe and he recorded walks that he made in the Trusthorpe area and in Lincoln. Many of the incidents which took place on this visit reappear in his book *Sons and Lovers*.

Lawrence made many return visits to Mablethorpe and a few to Skegness. The bleak landscape of the coast seems to have made a deep impression on him. Lincoln Cathedral features prominently in *The Rainbow*. After a long absence on the continent and in America, Lawrence returned to England in 1927 with his German-born wife and in August of that year stayed in Sutton-on-Sea. Lawrence died four years later in Venice.

FURTHER READING: Pinkney, T. *D. H. Lawrence* (1990)

Tommy LIDGETT (1844-1908)

Tommy Lidgett was born at Cherry Valley Farm, Rothwell, in 1844. At the age of five Tommy walked every day the seven miles to school at Caistor. To make the journey easier his father had made a hoop for him to bowl along the road. At the age of nine he earned twopence a day looking after cows in the lanes and bird scaring. When Tommy was twelve his parents moved to Thoresway Grange and he was then able to earn sixpence a day working with horses and sheep until he left home at the age of sixteen to work for a nearby farmer. He moved on to Beesby and attended the Primitive Methodist Chapel at Wold Newton.

In May 1854 Tommy set out to find work in Grimsby, walking the twelve miles. He found work as a docker before becoming a ship's cook. A life at sea wasn't for him and for five years he worked on the coal dock. In 1870 Lidgett joined a travelling auctioneer named Rees but in the following year decided to set up in business on his own account, first in Grimsby, then moving on to Gainsborough and finally to Lincoln.

Tommy Lidgett was a hard worker and he was able to open shops in Boston and Cleethorpes. He opened a shop and auction room in Lincoln and bought two houses in Grimsby. In 1889 his bank failed and this drove him to drink and smoking. To escape from depression which his losses had caused, he joined a fishing vessel at Grimsby and was at sea for two weeks. On his return to Lincoln he had a serious breakdown and was ill for over a year. He recovered and went to Sleaford where he started a business selling watches.

Tommy seems to have believed that his recovery was due to a group of friends who had met regularly to pray for him and he now became an ardent believer in the power of prayer. He became a particularly inspired preacher and spoke in many local chapels and in the market places. There are a number of reports of the performance of acts of kindness by Tommy which appear to have been divinely inspired. In 1908 Tommy Lidgett attended a Salvation Army Service and spoke for 45 minutes. The hymn that followed was *Say, are you ready if the Death Angel should call?* and half way through, Tommy dropped dead.

Tom a' LINCOLN

Tom a' Lincoln was a foundling child named after the place in which he was found and he was called Tom after the name by which the 'great bell' of the Cathedral was known.

The History of Tom a' Lincoln, the Red Rose Knight was published by Richard Johnson towards the end of the sixteenth century and in the book Tom is said to have been the illegitimate son of King Arthur. He married Anglitora the daughter of Prester John and had two sons known as 'the Blacke Knight and the Fayre Knight'. After many adventures the Red Rose Knight, as Tom became known, died and 'the King which then reigned was desirous to see the City of Lincoln where the Red Rose Knight was born. At whose coming into the city the great bell (called Tom a' Lincolne) was rung an hour, which as then was seldom done to any except Kings and renowned warriors, returning victoriously from bloody battels. Here builded they a most sumptuous minster'. The last line of the book reads as follows : 'Lincoln is, London was, York shall be'.

Tommy Lidgett

Thomas LINLEY Jnr. (1756-1778)

From an early age Thomas Linley Jnr. gave evidence of exceptional musical ability and was soon studying the violin under his father, Thomas. Thomas Linley, Snr. was director of the Drury Lane Oratorios and arranged and composed the music for some twenty plays, pantomimes and other entertainments. At the age of seven Thomas Linley Jnr. played a concerto at a concert in Bristol and in 1768 he went to Italy to study the violin with Nardini in Florence for about three years. Linley met Mozart there in April 1770 and returned to England in 1771 becoming a regular performer in concerts in Bath until 1776 when the family moved to London.

Whilst the family were the guests of the Duke of Ancaster at Grimsthorpe Castle in August 1778 Thomas Linley together with a Mr. Olivarez who is described as an 'Italian master' together with one other person decided to go on the lake in a sailing vessel. Unfortunately a sudden squall sprang up and the boat capsized. The three hung onto the boat for some time expecting help to arrive but eventually Linley decided to try to swim to the shore to fetch help. Foolishly, he did not remove his coat and boots and was drowned.

The parish register for Edenham, in which parish Grimsthorpe Castle lies, records the burial of 'Thos Lindly, bachelor' on 11 August 1778, apparently in the Ancaster vault in that church.

During the last five years of his life Linley composed an amazing quantity of music of the highest quality.

FURTHER READING: Sadie, S. *The New Grove Dictionary of Music and Musicians* Vol. 11 pp. 9-10. (1980); *Bath Chronicle* 13 August 1778.

William LOGSDAIL (1859-1944)

William Logsdail was born on 25 May 1859 in the close of Lincoln, in a house on the north side of Exchequergate. His father, George Logsdail, was verger of the Cathedral for over fifty years and William had five brothers and one sister.

From a very early age William made the Cathedral the subject for drawings and paintings. He could draw before he could write! In a manuscript book of memoirs he said that he earned his first pennies by conducting visitors up the central tower of the Cathedral.

William was a pupil at the Lincoln School (now Lincoln Christ's Hospital School) and then studied at the Lincoln School of Art. It was intended that he should become an architect but he was encouraged at the Art School to become a painter. He had a particular friend at the Art School, Frank Bramley, with whom he travelled on painting and sketching tours, spending one vacation in a farmhouse at Studley near Redditch. In 1877 at the age of 18, William went to London and rented a room on the corner of Tottenham Street and Charlotte Street. He spent much time in and around Westminster Cathedral and drawing from life at the Hogarth Club. A year later he went to Antwerp, where he studied for nearly two years. Upon return to England he went back to London for a short time before travelling to Venice. In

1883 he toured the Balkans, Egypt and the Holy Land but Venice remained his home, from which he visited London for the Royal Academy exhibitions.

In 1892 he married Mary Ashman of Necton, Norfolk and they returned to Venice, where they were to remain for a further eight years. In 1900 William and Mary Logsdail with their three children, Mary, Edward and Stuart, left Venice to return to England but the journey took two years as they made a lengthy visit to Taormina, Sicily on the way. On their eventual arrival in England the family made their home in London, where they remained until 1922 when they moved to the village of Noke in Oxfordshire.

William was a prolific painter and at the age of fifteen whilst at Lincoln School of Art he won a Gold Medal for the best work of all the schools of art in England. At seventeen years of age four of his entries for the Royal Academy were hung and sold. In all his life he only had one picture rejected by the Academy. At the age of eighteen he painted fourteen pictures in North Wales and these were sold at prices ranging from £2 to thirty-five guineas each. In 1877 he recorded that his receipts from picture sales up to that date totalled £530. He was able to support himself by painting and his work achieved great popularity. *The Fish Market*, which he had painted in Antwerp and exhibited at the Royal Academy, was bought by Queen Victoria for Osborne House.

It was during the period 1907 to 1914 after his return to England that his work received most attention and it is some measure of his reputation that several pictures with a forged signature appeared on the market. Following the success of his portrait of his daughter Mary, exhibited at the Royal Academy in 1907, he received many commissions for which he charged a fee of six hundred pounds. He found this work less strenuous because he could choose his sitters from a long list, knowing that after the completion of one portrait another would immediately follow. His painting career can be summarised by periods as follows: up to 1907 architectural and subject paintings ; 1907 to 1922 portraiture; 1922 to 1937 Oxford paintings and flower studies. From 1937 until his death in 1944 he painted little, preferring to tend his garden at Noke.

Edward MAKINS (died 1886)

TORKSEY NED

Edward Makins or 'Torksey Ned' as he was usually known, must have been a somewhat remarkable character. He died in Lincoln Union Workhouse on 21 May 1886 and it is not many inmates of a workhouse whose death is recorded by an obituary in the local newspaper. In the obituary of 'Torksey Ned' which appeared in the *Lincolnshire Chronicle* he was said to be a 'great big hulking fellow who followed the casual calling of a drover. The butt of every urchin who spotted him with his business-like ash plant, his boots usually unlaced, his soft felt hat usually tied beneath his chin and his coat usually buttoned up one hole out of true, with his hostile grumbling and his ash-plant ever ready to be hurled viciously after some suspected person within range. He lumbered heavily after the stick which nimble youths took advantage of and kicked further away as they put thumb to nose and ran'.

The obituary continues: 'This well known eccentric individual died in Lincoln Union Workhouse on Thursday morning - formerly a cattle drover and there were few markets and fairs in the district at which his burly form was not at one time seen. Of late years, however, when not an inmate of Lincoln Workhouse, he executed various odd jobs which came his way. His reward in many cases was a "drop of beer" and occasionally this questionable mode of remuneration affected him so much that he had to appear before the Magistrates. His invariable reply to the charge was a cry of "Oh, my poor head, it's my poor head that's done it" He was a harmless old fellow and frequently the butt of thoughtless youths, some of whom, after he had received much provocation, would at times experience a smarting knowledge of the power of the stick which he usually carried. The soubriquet "Torksey Ned" was acquired because he was a native of Torksey or its locality'.

Shortly before Makins' death a plaster statuette was modelled from life by Mr. J. C. Divell and was presented to the City and County Museum in 1936. Torksey Ned's fame must have been considerable, for a postcard taken from a studio portrait was printed.

Robert MANNYNG (c1268-c1340)

All that is known of Robert Mannyng's early life is that he was a native of Bourne and for this reason he is sometimes known as Robert de Brunne. He is known to have entered Sempringham Priory in 1288 and it was here that he wrote his best known work, *Handlyng Synne*, in 1303. Mannyng may have studied at Cambridge University at the same time as Robert Bruce, later King of Scotland, and his two brothers.

In 1338 Robert Manning was resident at Six Hills Priory and he appears to have been seventy years of age at that time. Mannyng is best known for his free translation of the *Manuel des Pechnez* of William of Waddington. This work, which Mannyng did not hesitate to amend as he saw fit, was published under the title *Handlyng Synne* and gives an important picture of social life of the late thirteenth and early fourteenth centuries. He also wrote a *Chronicle of England* which is a collection of the works of others recording events from 'the death of Cadwallender to the end of King Edward I reign'. Also sometimes ascribed to Mannyng is *Meditacynes of ye Soper of our Lorde Ihesus and also of Ihesus and also of hys Passyn and eke of ye paynes of hys swete moder, Mayden Marye ye whyche made from Latyn Benoventure Cadyball.*

Neville MARRINER (1924-   )

Neville Marriner was born in Lincoln on 15 April 1924 and is the son of Herbert Henry and Ethel May Marriner. His father was a gifted teacher of the piano, violin and voice. Herbert Marriner was also a choral conductor of some distinction. Ethel Marriner sang in her husband's choral groups and Neville says that she 'diligently supervised my practice'. Neville Marriner was educated at Lincoln School (now Christ's Hospital School) and the Royal College of Music, where he obtained his ARCM.

He taught music at Eton College and was appointed Professor at the Royal College of Music in 1950. Neville Marriner was Music Director of the Los Angeles Chamber Orchestra from 1968 until 1977 and was Director of the Stuttgart Radio Symphony Orchestra from 1984 until 1989. He was Artistic Director of the South Bank Summer Festival from 1975 until 1977 and the Meadow Bank Festival from 1977 to 1979, Detroit Symphony Orchestra from 1979 until 1983 and Musical Director of the Barbican Summer Festival from 1985 until 1987.

Neville Marriner was awarded the C.B.E in 1979 and was knighted in 1985. He founded the Academy of St. Martin in the Fields in 1956 and has been Director from its foundation. Sir Neville has now conducted all the major symphony orchestras world-wide.

William MARSHALL (1812-1861)

William Marshall, who was born in 1812, was the son of John Marshall, a block and tackle manufacturer of Gainsborough. At an early age he was sent to Manchester to train as a millwright with William Fairbairns.

In 1834 he married Eliza Dickenson and they set up home in Stalybridge and on 17 May 1836 their first son James was born. Four years later they moved to Amcotts and a second son, Henry, was born. In 1840 William Marshall was appointed by Fairbairn to represent the firm in St. Petersburg, which was then the capital city of Russia. Eliza died in 1845 and William returned with his two sons to Manchester. In 1847 he married Frances Grandage.

In 1848 William acquired the small engineering works of William Garland in Gainsborough. His advertisement at that time describes the business as that of a millwright and engineer. In 1849 the firm won a prize for a new portable threshing machine at the Royal Agricultural Show in Norwich. This was the first of many awards to the Company for agricultural innovations which they introduced over the next 135 years.

William's second wife Frances died in 1859 and William himself died on 16 June 1861. The firm continued to prosper under William's sons James and Henry and achieved a reputation for quality and reliability.

William MARWOOD (1820-1883)

William Marwood was born at Goulceby in 1820 and became a shoemaker in Horncastle, working close to the parish church. He was appointed public hangman and his first engagement was at Lincoln in 1871. Marwood managed to keep his secondary occupation a secret for some time even from his wife but when the news eventually came into the open he was ostracised in the town. Marwood became very proud of his work and he displayed in his workshop coils of rope with which he had carried out executions. Amongst his 'clients' were such notorious criminals as Charles Peace, Dr. Lamson and Kate Webster. It was Marwood who perfected the humane 'long drop'.

William Marwood performed his last hanging in London two weeks before he died on 4 September 1883.

William MONSON (1569-1643)

William Monson was the third son of Sir John Monson of South Carlton and was born in 1529. At the age of sixteen he 'went to sea without his parents' knowledge'. He had an exciting introduction to Elizabethan naval life when his ship came into contact with a Spanish vessel in the Bay of Biscay. The Englishmen boarded the Spanish ship but were stranded when the English captain had to pull away. However, the Englishmen won the day and the Spanish ship was brought back to Plymouth.

During the repulsion of the Spanish Armada, at the age of nineteen, Lieutenant Monson was in command of the warship *Charles* and in the following year he captained a ship in the Earl of Cumberland's expedition to the Azores. In 1596 Monson took part in an expedition to Cadiz and was one of the landing party. As a result of this he was knighted by the Earl of Essex in the market place of the fallen city.

After a number of adventures, on the accession of James I Sir William was appointed Admiral of the Narrow Seas, which made him responsible for the safety of the English Channel and the Irish Sea. He retained this appointment for twelve years and in 1614 embarked on a campaign to rid the coastal waters of the scourge of pirates. This was a particularly successful enterprise. Monson had long campaigned for the reform of the Navy and had incurred the enmity of a number of his contemporaries and especially Lord Howard.

It was alleged that he had taken part in a conspiracy to murder Sir Thomas Overbury and, although he was acquitted, he was retired from the Navy. For twenty years he was unemployed but as a result of his support of the unpopular Ship Money Tax he was recalled to service by Charles I. After service against the combined fleets of France and the Netherlands he retired and began writing the *Naval Tracts* which recorded important facts about the naval strength of England at that time.

Admiral Sir William Monson died in 1643 and was buried in St. Martin-in-the-Fields.

Fynes MORYSON (1566-1629)

Fynes Moryson was born in 1566 and was the third son of Thomas Moryson of Cadeby, the Member of Parliament for Grimsby in 1572, 1584, 1586 and 1588-9. His mother was the daughter of Thomas Moigne of Willingham, who had been Recorder of Lincoln and the only gentleman to have been executed after the Lincolnshire Rising of 1536. The unusual Christian name 'Fynes' may have been in honour of Edward Fiennes, Lord Clinton and Saye, who was Lord Lieutenant of Lincolnshire at the time Moryson was born.

Nothing is known of Moryson's early schooling but he graduated Bachelor of Arts at Cambridge in 1570 and became a Fellow of Peterhouse in the following year. He was awarded the degree of Master of Arts at Oxford University and in 1598 he returned to live with his sisters Faith and Jane, who were both married and lived in the vicinity of Healing.

Moryson travelled widely and at the age of 25 he left England to travel in Europe. He narrowly escaped capture by pirates at Dunkirk. In his book *Ten yeeres Travel through the Twelve Dominions of Germany, Bohmerland, Sweizerland, Netherland, Denmarke, Poland,*

Italy, Turkey, France, England, Scotland and Ireland published in 1617, he tells of many escapes from difficult situations. It appears that many of these escapades arose because of his curiosity and recklessness. Not content with these travels and adventures he soon set off again for the Near East with his brother Henry. Whilst in Antioch, both brothers were very ill with dysentery and Fynes returned to England when Henry died.

He became secretary to Lord Mountjoy and travelled with him to Ireland when he was sent to put down the Tyrone rebellion.

Isaac NEWTON (1642-1727)

Isaac Newton was born on Christmas Day 1642 at Woolsthorpe Manor, Colsterworth. His father, who was lord of the manor, died three months before Isaac was born and his mother re-married but was widowed again by the time Isaac reached the age of eleven. He had a step-brother and two step-sisters. Although young Isaac was a delicate child he was very dextrous with his hands and there is a sun-dial in Colsterworth church which he made at the age of nine. He attended King's School, Grantham lodging with a local apothecary, and made a wooden clock worked by water which told the time for the household.

Isaac became head boy at King's and went on to Trinity College, Cambridge where he soon demonstrated his ability and was able to answer quickly problems which his tutors had anticipated would take many hours to discuss. Newton was deeply religious and he made translations of biblical histories and questioned errors in the original texts. Newton was absent minded and would sit for hours deep in thought and often missed meals. It was said that he would walk home for miles leading his horse which he had forgotten to mount! When living in London, he exasperated a lady who lived opposite by sitting at his open window blowing soap bubbles from a clay pipe completely engrossed, watching the colour and light as the bubbles floated across the street!

Isaac Newton became Master of the Mint and his inventions vastly improved the manufacture of coins. Queen Anne conferred a knighthood on him in 1705 and she spoke of him as 'the greatest genius of the land'. When he died at the age of 85 he was buried with great ceremony in Westminster Abbey. The inscription on a marble tablet which was placed over the fireplace in the room in which Newton was born at Woolsthorpe Manor reads as follows: 'Sir Isaac Newton, son of Isaac Newton, (Lord of the Manor of Woolsthorpe) was born in this room December 25th 1642. "Nature and nature's laws lay hid in night, God said, 'Let Newton be', and all was light"- Pope'

Newton summed up his own life as follows : 'I do not know what I may appear to the world; but to myself I seem to have been only like a boy playing on the sea-shore and diverting in now and then finding a smoother pebble or a prettier shell than ordinary whilst the great ocean of truth lay all undiscovered before me'.

Lord Byron in his poem *Don Juan* included the following two verses in praise of Newton :

'When Newton saw an apple fall, he found
In that slight startle from his contemplation -
'Tis said (for I'll not answer above ground
For any sage's creed) that the earth turn'd round
In a most natural whirl called "gravitation";
And this is the sole mortal who could grapple
Since Adam, with a fall, or with an apple.

Man fell with apples and with apples rose
If this be true for us we deem the mode
In which Sir Isaac Newton could disclose
Through the then unpaved stars the turnpike road,
A thing to counterbalance human woes;
For ever since immortal man hath glowed
With all kinds of mechanics and full soon
Steam-engines will conduct him to the moon'.

FURTHER READING: McTavish, D. *Isaac Newton* (1990)

Tom OTTER (died 1807)

Thomas Temporal alias Otter was a labourer working on the enclosure of Swanpool, Lincoln. He became friendly with a young local girl and she had a child by him. As was usual at that time, the magistrates ordered them to marry and the ceremony took place on 4 November 1806 at Hykeham Church with Otter standing between two parish constables.

Afterwards the pair walked along the road to Saxilby and near Drinsey Nook, whilst his wife was resting, Tom took a fencing stake and beat her to death. Otter was already married and this may have been the reason for the murder. Tom was soon caught, tried and hanged. His body was taken and placed on a gibbet near the place where the murder took place and the spot is still known as Gibbet Wood. A bluetit built a nest between the jaw bones of the skeleton and this is the incident on which the following riddle is based : 'There were nine tongues within one head / The tenth went out to seek for bread / To feed the living within the dead'

It is said that the fencing-stake with which the murder was committed was kept at the Sun Inn, Saxilby but each year on the anniversary of the murder it disappeared. The stake always re-appeared on the footpath near the spot where the murder had been committed. This footpath over the years had become known as 'Tom Otter's Lane'. The disappearing trick was repeated each year even though the stake was moved to various hostelries in the area. Eventually the Bishop of Lincoln ordered that the stake was to be burned and this was done on Minster Green!

Although this was the end of the stake, there is a little known sequel to the story. It seems that on his death-bed one Dunkerly confessed to the parson that when he was a young lad he was given to following couples and spying on them. On the day of the murder he had followed

Otter and his wife and had witnessed the tragedy. He ran away from the scene in terror and never mentioned the incident to anyone, but each year during the night before the anniversary of the murder, Tom and his 'wife' appeared and took him to the Inn where the fencing stake was kept. He was made to take the stake from its fastenings on the wall and carry it to Gibbet Wood, where the murder was re-enacted!

Thomas PAINE (1737-1809)

Thomas Paine was an excise officer who was born in Thetford in 1737. Paine's involvement with the excise began in Grantham and on 8 August 1764 he was posted to Alford were he had an office in an upstairs room at the Windmill Inn. Alford was at that time a centre for smuggling (or 'free-trading', as the smugglers preferred to call it). Wool was illegally exported from Lincolnshire beaches at night and alcohol and tea were imported. Paine's attitude was to discourage rather than punish smuggling and within a year of moving to Alford he was dismissed from the excise service but was eventually reinstated after moving to Lewes in Sussex.

In 1774 Thomas Paine emigrated to America and quickly became an influential writer and editor. It is Thomas Paine who is credited with the conception of the name 'United States of America' and he was a friend of Benjamin Franklin and George Washington. He became Secretary to the Department for Foreign Affairs and Clerk to the Assembly of Pennsylvania. He left America for France and wrote *The Rights of Man, The Age of Reason* and *Common Sense* which are still in print. He returned to America and died on 8 June 1809.

Thomas Paine is very highly regarded in America as one of the founders of the United States and on 4 July 1981 a plaque commemorating his Alford connection was erected at the Windmill Hotel in the town's market place.

FURTHER READING: Ayer, A. J. *Thomas Paine* (1988)

Alfred PICCAVER (1884-1958)

Alfred Piccaver was born on 5 February 1884 at Long Sutton and was the son of a chemist who emigrated to America when Alfred was a young boy.

Young Alfred started his working life as an electrical engineer at Edison in New York and whenever he could he attended the Metropolitan Opera House. It was there that he heard the great Caruso. Alfred used to sing at his workbench and the director of the Opera House was so impressed with his voice that he helped him to obtain a grant to enable him to have singing lessons. In 1907 Alfred Piccaver was given an audition by the musical director of the Prague Opera House, who engaged him to sing in Gounod's *Romeo and Juliet*.

Although his lyrical, gentle and mellow tenor voice attracted great attention, Piccaver had a lot to learn and he moved to Italy, where he was trained by Caruso's teacher, Rosario. Piccaver had to sing to earn a living and to pay for his lessons so he joined the Italian Battistini Stagione travelling with them to Vienna in 1910. He sang the part of the Duke in Verdi's *Rigoletto* and never looked back, staying in Vienna until 1937.

Piccaver had a tremendous range and amongst his successes were Cavaradossi, Radames, Don Jose, Bajazzo and Lohengrin. He sang in *Manon*, in *Butterfly*, in *The Magic Flute*, *Ariadne* and *Andrea Chénier*. He and Lotte Lehmann sang in the European premiere of Puccini's *Girl from the Golden West*. Alfred Piccaver was a keen sportsman and it was said that his contract allowed him to cancel a performance if it interfered with an international football or boxing match! When he died in Vienna in 1958, such was the fame of this Lincolnshire-born opera singer that he was given a state funeral. The whole of the government of the day attended his funeral and the Vienna Philharmonic Orchestra played the Funeral March from Beethoven's *Eroica* Symphony.

Steve RACE (1921-   )

Steve Race is probably best known as the chairman and compiler of *My Music*, the radio and television programme which ran from 1966 until 1994. Steve was born on 1 April 1921 in St. Catherine's Lincoln and soon indicated his future career by improvising on the family piano. By the age of six he was able to reproduce virtually any music he heard.

It was soon realised that he ought to have formal music lessons and his first teacher was Miss Elsie M. Harrison who, as well as teaching him basic piano playing, wisely encouraged him to study gramophone recordings. At the age of eight he took to xylophone playing, giving concerts in local chapels and halls. He also played the organ for services in the chapel of the Lawn Mental Hospital.

In 1929 he became a pupil at Lincoln School (now Lincoln Christ's Hospital School) and became friendly with Alex Cullen, with whom he formed a jazz duo: Alex on the drums and Steve at the piano. The partnership faded when the future Professor Cullen became more interested in science than in music. A schoolboy band was formed which the young Neville Marriner applied to join. At the age of fifteen Steve auditioned before the Lincoln-born Professor Frederick Jackson and was accepted as a student at the Royal Academy of Music of which he is now a Fellow.

Soon after war was declared he volunteered for the Royal Air Force and served in various parts of Britain. In June 1944 he married Clair Leng of Lincoln and soon afterwards began his broadcasting career as a pianist and a record presenter. Following his demobilization in 1946, after spells with the bands of Lew Stone and Cyril Stapleton, he formed his own band, performing regularly on radio and television.

He has contributed articles for newspapers and magazines world-wide while his published books include an autobiography and *The Two Worlds of Joseph Race*, the story of his grandfather's life in China. For the entire long run as chairman of *My Music*, Steve set the questions and he estimates the total at over 15,000. He has composed the music for documentary films, television plays and commercial 'jingles', while his set of orchestral variations was performed under Sir John Barbarolli by the Hallé Orchestra. The best known of his compositions remains the tune which he named *Nicola*, after his daughter. It won the Ivor Novello Award in 1962.

Steve's musical interests have always been divided between classical, popular and jazz music. His recreations include reading history, studying seventeenth century Dutch painting, and 'a tendency to argue about politics'. He lives with his wife Lonny, a former BBC producer, in the Chiltern Hills. Steve Race was awarded the OBE in 1992 and is a Freeman of the City of London.

FURTHER READING: Race, S. *Musician at Large* (1979)

William Robert ROBERTSON (1860-1933)

William Robertson was born at Welbourn on 29 January 1860 and was the son of the village tailor and postmaster, Thomas Charles Robertson. Young Will was educated at the village school, together with his two older brothers and four sisters. He was an avid reader and had an aptitude for drawing but was also interested in geography and maps. After leaving school, Will became garden boy at the Rectory but he soon moved on to Ashby-de-la-Launde, where he worked for the eccentric parson.

In 1875 Will Robertson became footman with the Cardigan family at Deene Park in Northamptonshire and it was here that his enthusiasm for the army first developed. He worked for the seventh Earl, who was Colonel of the 11th Hussars, and had led the ill-fated Charge of the Light Brigade at Balaclava in 1854.

When almost eighteen, four years after leaving Welbourn, William took the Queen's shilling and was posted to Aldershot for training. He became a Lance Corporal in May 1881, Sergeant in January 1882 and Troop Sergeant Major in March 1885 when still only 25. In 1886 William decided to make the attempt to gain a commission, which was no easy matter at that time, but in 1888 he was gazetted Second Lieutenant in the Dragoon Guards. His first officer's uniform was made by his father and in a letter to his mother he said 'I find that the clothes Father made me compare very favourably with any others here and feel very thankful for the trouble he has taken and hope to repay him one day'. William Robertson was posted to India in December 1888 and after only two years qualified as an interpreter in five Indian languages!

In a letter to his father he said 'In the midst of the highest society one's thoughts fly back to Welbourn and its well remembered little bits of domestic life of my early days. There I see real love whilst here amid all the gaiety and apparent friendship, I feel that were I not an officer, tomorrow there would perhaps be none to recognise me...'

In 1895 William Robertson was awarded the Distinguished Service Order and promoted to Captain, seven years after his first commission. Captain Robertson was the first ranker officer to attend the Staff College at Camberley from which he graduated in 1899. In 1907 he was appointed Chief of Staff with the rank of Brigadier-General.

In 1910 Robertson became Commandant of the Staff College with the rank of Major-General and in 1912 he was knighted. In 1914 Major-General Sir William Robertson was appointed Quartermaster-General to the British Expeditionary Force and in November 1915 he was appointed Chief of Staff to Sir John French. Four weeks later he became Chief of the Imperial General Staff under Lord Kitchener. In 1918 a disagreement with Lloyd George led to his retirement from the Army with the rank of Field Marshal. It was fitting that the Memorial to the eleven men from Welbourn who gave their lives in the Great War was unveiled by Field Marshal Robertson.

William Robertson died in 1933, seventy-three years after his humble birth. A memorial tablet bearing his Coat-of-Arms and motto 'Fight the Good Fight' is in Welbourn Parish Church, inscribed as follows: 'Sacred to the Memory of Field Marshal SIR WILLIAM ROBERT ROBERTSON, Baronet G.C.B., G.C.M.G., G.C.V.O., D.S.O., D.C.L. (Oxon), L.L.D.(Cantab)., Born in this Parish 29th January, 1860. Died 12th February, 1933. This tablet, representing a portion of a memorial fund raised by Lincolnshire men and old comrades and friends in all parts of the British Empire, is here placed to perpetuate the remembrance of a great soldier who, by his own indomitable energy, resource, skill and judgement, accomplished the distinction of rising from a Trooper in the 16th Lancers to the rank of Field Marshal. His varied and distinguished services included the North West Frontier of India 1895; South Africa 1899-1900; Commandant of the Staff College 1910-13. In the Great War, Quartermaster General and Chief of the General Staff 1914-15 and Chief of the Imperial General Staff 1915-18; also General Officer Commanding in Chief of the Army of the Rhine 1919-20. In all things to all men and a high example. REQUIESCAT IN PACE'

Frederick John ROBINSON (1782-1859)

Frederick Robinson was the second son of Thomas Robinson, second baron Grantham, and was born on 30 October 1782. He was educated at Harrow School and St John's College, Cambridge graduating with the degree of Master of Arts in 1802. He entered Lincoln's Inn on 7 May 1802 but was never called to the Bar.

From 1804 until 1806 he was private secretary to the Earl of Hardwicke and was elected Member of Parliament for the borough of Carlow at the General Election of November 1806. At the General Election in the following May he was elected member for Ripon, which he represented for over twenty years. In 1809 he was appointed Under Secretary for the Colonies but relinquished that office later that year. Robinson held a number of other Government posts, including joint Paymaster-General, President of the Board of Trade and on 31 January 1823 was appointed Chancellor of the Exchequer. On the death of Canning in August 1827, the King asked Robinson to form a Cabinet but he was succeeded as Prime Minister by the Duke of Wellington on 8 January 1828.

Wellington did not offer him any ministerial post but his successor, Lord Grey, appointed Robinson Secretary of State for War and later, Lord Privy Seal. When Sir Robert Peel succeeded Grey, Robinson was appointed President of the Board of Trade.

Robinson was created Viscount Goderich of Nocton on 28 April 1827 and in April 1833 he was created Earl of Ripon. Robinson was described as an amiable, upright but irresolute man and he was given when Chancellor of the Exchequer the nick-name 'Prosperity Robinson' and when Secretary for the Colonies 'Goody Goderich', presumably for his vehement support for the abolition of slavery. He was also said to have been 'probably the weakest prime minister who ever had office in this country'. Frederick Robinson, Earl of Ripon died on 28 January 1859 and was buried at Nocton.

Joseph RUSTON (1835-1897)

Joseph Ruston was born at Chatteris, Cambridgeshire, in 1835 and was the son of a farmer and Wesleyan local preacher. Joseph was sent to the Wesley College in Sheffield at the age of sixteen but soon left to become an apprentice at the Washington Foundry in Sheffield. The main product of the foundry was cutlery.

On 1 January 1857, Joseph Ruston went into partnership with Burton and Proctor of Lincoln, a firm of millwrights and general smiths. From this time, the firm began to expand and in July 1857 Burton was bought out. The firm began to manufacture portable steam engines and four years later Proctor retired. This was the beginnings of a firm which has become world famous and has only recently dropped the name of Ruston and changed its title to English Gas Turbines.

FURTHER READING: Newman, B. *One Hundred Years of Good Company* (1957)

Malcolm SARGENT (1895-1967)

Harold Malcolm Watts Sargent is usually said to have been born in Stamford but, in fact, this is not the case. He was born rather unexpectedly at Ashford in Kent where his mother was on a visit to a family friend. However, he was soon brought to the family home at 24 Wharf Road, Stamford and, even after he became famous and spent much of his time in London, he seems to have regarded the town as his home.

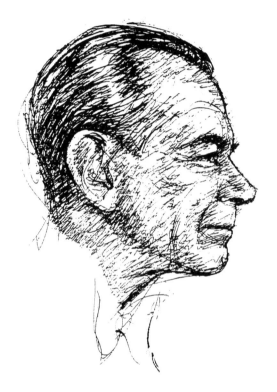

His mother Agnes had been a matron at Stamford High School for Girls before her marriage and his father Henry was a clerk and eventually manager of a coal office in Red Lion Square. He was also a piano and violin player and organist at St. John's Church. It was his father who decided that Malcolm should have piano lessons with Mrs Frances Tinkler. It is said that young Malcolm was so keen to practice on the piano at home that he would rush in after school and start playing without even taking his gloves off! Malcolm Sargent's early conducting was with a group of Miss Tinkler's pupils. At the age of three, young Malcolm joined the infants department at the National School in Stamford and shortly before his sixth birthday he transferred to the Blue Coat School. When he reached the age of twelve he became a pupil at Stamford Grammar School, where he was allowed to practise his piano playing instead of taking part in sporting activities.

After leaving School at the age of fifteen, he continued his piano lessons and taught himself transposition. He could play many pieces from memory in any key. In July 1912 he was successful in the examinations of the Royal College of Organists and so became, at the age of sixteen, an Associate Member of that body. His first experience as a conductor was with a group of Frances Tinkler's pupils in 1909 when the Stamford Operatic Society was rehearsing *Yeomen of the Guard*, on one occasion the regular conductor was unable to attend and Malcolm was asked to fill the breach. This was the turning point in his musical career and his first public appearance as conductor was on 24 and 25 July 1912, at a pageant to commemorate the visit of Queen Elizabeth I to Burleigh in 1565. Frances Tinkler said on one occasion that Malcolm Sargent 'had the assurance of Old Nick' and no doubt this accounts at least in part for his success as a conductor.

Malcolm Sargent was taught first by his father at St. John's to play the organ and then by the organist at All Saints' Church, Stamford. In the autumn of 1912 he was articled to the organist of Peterborough Cathedral, travelling each day by train. In 1914 he was awarded the degree of Bachelor of Music by Durham University and in the same year he was appointed organist of St. Mary's parish church, Melton Mowbray. He was the youngest of the 151 candidates for the post! In 1915 he was appointed music master at the Grammar School in Melton and when the conductor of the town band was called-up Sargent took over. In early 1918 he also received his calling-up papers but was released soon after the armistice in November of that year and he returned to Melton Mowbray. The following year he became, at the age of 24, the youngest ever Doctor of Music.

Another turning point in Malcolm Sargent's career came on 3 February 1921. Sir Henry Wood had been invited to bring the Queen's Hall Orchestra to Leicester and the organising committee had asked Sargent to produce a composition. Two weeks before the date of the concert Wood complained that the piece hadn't been received and Sargent would have to conduct it himself if it was to be performed. The title of the piece was *Impressions on a Windy Day* and Sargent conducted it with great success. Sir Henry invited him to repeat the performance at the Proms on 11 October in the same year. This was the real start of his remarkable musical career and Malcolm Sargent was an extremely popular conductor. He received a knighthood in 1947. The biography by Charles Reid records his achievements in detail but despite all the honours he received he never forgot Stamford and when he died on 3 October 1967 he was buried in Stamford Cemetery. His death was only two weeks after he had spoken with great courage at The Last Night of the Proms. Sir Malcolm's tombstone is inscribed 'We thank Thee who has revealed Thyself in great music, and for giving us understanding of it.'

FURTHER READING: Reid, Charles. *Malcolm Sargent: A Biography* (1968)

Charles SIBTHORP (1783-1855)

Charles de Laet Waldo Sibthorp was the second son of Colonel Humphrey Waldo Sibthorp of Canwick Hall and he inherited the estate after his brother, Coningsby, who was the Member of Parliament for Lincoln, died in 1822.

Charles matriculated at Brasenose College, Oxford in 1801 and entered the army soon afterwards. He saw service in the Peninsular War as a captain in the Royal Irish Dragoon Guards and married an Irish heiress, Maria Ponsonby Tottenham. In August 1824 he was involved in a duel with Dr. Edward Charlesworth, who was well known for his work with the mentally ill. The shooting of the two duellists was erratic and both left the scene unhurt!

Sibthorp succeeded his brother as Member of Parliament for Lincoln in 1826 but six years later he was unseated by Edward Bulwer-Lytton, the well-known novelist. Only two years later Sibthorp regained the seat which he held until his death, a period of thirty years. It was said that Sibthorp was a diehard who set his feet against anything likely to alter the established order of things. Charles Dickens, in *Sketches by Boz,* described him as a ferocious looking gentleman with a huge black moustache, 'the most amusing person in the House' who was frequently to be seen striding about clasping a bundle of important looking papers which in fact were years old and in no way related to the business in hand!

When Lord Melbourne, the Prime Minister, proposed to make an allowance of fifty thousand pounds a year to Prince Albert on his marriage to Queen Victoria, Colonel Sibthorp spoke vigorously against this. This was apparently because the Prince was a German and surprisingly Sibthorp gained considerable support. The allowance was reduced to thirty thousand pounds. This did not please Queen Victoria and she vowed never to visit Lincoln as long as Sibthorp remained its representative! Sibthorp opposed the plans for the Great Exhibition of 1851 because it was the idea of Prince Albert. True to his principles, Sibthorp opposed the spread of the railways which were in his opinion 'public frauds and private robberies'.

This eccentric and overbearing Lincolnshire character died in London in 1855 and was buried at Canwick.

John SMITH (1580-1631)

John Smith was baptised at Willoughby near Alford on 6 January 1579-80 and was the son of George and Alice Smith. His father died in 1596 and John went to seek his fortune by joining the French army. In 1598 he joined the insurgents in the Low Countries. In about 1600 John Smith returned to Willoughby for a short time to study the theory of war. Later that year he again left Lincolnshire to seek adventure and entered the service of the Archduke of Austria. At the Battle of Rothenthurm he was captured and sold as a slave but escaped and returned to England in 1605.

On 19 December 1606 he emigrated with 105 others to found the colony of Virginia. Smith was a member of the Council appointed to administer the colony and proved himself an energetic and effective leader. On an expedition in search of food in December 1607 Smith was taken prisoner and released through the intervention of the Indian princess Pocahontas. The well-known story is possibly, at least in part, legendary.

John Smith became head of the colony on 10 September 1608 although, in fact, he appears to have been from the beginning its guiding spirit. It was through his influence that order and industry was instilled into the settlers who built houses and a church and began to support themselves through agriculture and fishing. In the summer of 1608, Smith explored the coastline of the colony and constructed a map of Chesapeake Bay. Captain Smith had maintained good relations with the natives but in 1609 a fresh party of colonists arrived and dissension arose.

An accidental injury caused him to leave the colony and return to England. However, he had established the solid foundations upon which Virginia could expand and prosper. In 1615 whilst returning to New England he was taken prisoner by the French but was set free and returned to England. In 1617 he made a further attempt to return to New England but the voyage was again abandoned because of bad weather.

Captain John Smith died in June 1631 and was buried in St. Sepulchre's Church, London.

FURTHER READING: Barbour, P. L. *The three worlds of Captain John Smith* (1964)

William STUKELEY (1687-1765)

William Stukeley was born at Holbeach on 7 November 1687 and was the son of John Stukeley, an attorney. He was educated at the Free School in Holbeach and spent much of his spare time in the woods, reading and collecting plants. Young William collected coins, learned wood carving and some astrology. On 7 November 1703 he was admitted to Corpus Christi College, Cambridge and was awarded the degree of Bachelor of Medicine on 21 January 1708. It is said that whilst at College he would steal dogs in order to dissect them!

On leaving Cambridge he studied anatomy and medicine in London and in 1710 he went into medical practice in Boston. In 1717 Stukeley returned to London and in the following year he was elected to a fellowship of the Royal Society. Stukeley was a founder member when the Society of Antiquaries was established in 1718 and was secretary for nine years. On 7 July 1719 he was awarded the degree of Doctor of Medicine by Cambridge University and in the following year he was admitted to fellowship of the College of Physicians. In 1722 Stukeley was elected a member of the Spalding Gentlemen's Society and in 1745 he founded the Brazen Nose Society.

William Stukeley married Frances Williamson of Allington in 1728 and they had three daughters. Frances died in 1737 and in 1739 Stukeley married Elizabeth Gale of York. With friends he went on long antiquarian tours throughout England and recorded many ancient buildings. A book on Stonehenge was published by him in 1740.

In 1726 Stukeley set up in medical practice in Grantham and in 1729 he was ordained and presented to the living of All Saints, Stamford, where he remained until 1748. Stukeley published *Palaeographia Sacra* in 1736. He intended the book to show 'how heathen mythology is derived from sacred history...' In 1739 he was presented to the living of Somerby but resigned this and the Stamford living in 1747 so that he could accept the living of St. George the Martyr in London. It is said that in April 1764 Stukeley postponed a service for an hour so that the congregation could witness an eclipse of the sun! Strangely enough at the age of

76, after he had been forced to wear spectacles, he preached from the text 'Now we see through a glass darkly' on the evil of too much study!

William Stukeley died on 27 February 1765 and was buried at East Ham.

FURTHER READING: Piggott, S. *William Stukeley* (1950)

Sarah SWIFT (1854-1937)

Sarah Anne Swift was born on 22 November 1854 at Kirton Skeldyke. She was the daughter of a family who had farmed at Blossom Hall Farm from the mid-eighteenth century. However, the family appears to have moved from Kirton in the mid-nineteenth century to the Red House at Donington Wykes, where Sarah spent her childhood.

In 1877 Sarah, after completing her education at the Cowley School in Donington, entered the Dundee Royal Infirmary as a probationer nurse and completed her training on 31 October 1879. She was appointed Assistant Matron of the Dundee Home for Incurables and remained there until 1886. In 1887 she was Ward Superintendent of the City Infirmary, Liverpool and in 1888 and 1889 Night Superintendent of the London Fever Hospital. She then decided to study nursing in the United States of America before accepting the post of Superintendent of Nursing at the British Seamen's Hospital in Constantinople, returning to England in 1890.

In December of that year she entered Guy's Hospital as a 'Lady pupil'. This was because, at that time, nurses were divided into two groups — a small body of lady pupils and a larger number of other nurses. The lady pupils usually came from well-to-do homes, were well educated and paid a considerable fee for their training. After completing her training Sarah was appointed Assistant Matron at Guy's and Lady Superintendent of Guy's Trained Nurses Institute which was an institute for private nurses with its headquarters in St. Thomas's Street. In 1900 Sarah Swift was appointed Matron, a post which she held until her retirement in 1909.

However, Sarah Swift's retirement did not last long and her nursing experience was called on at the outbreak of war in 1914, when she was appointed Matron-in-Chief of the Joint War Committee of the British Red Cross Society and the Order of St. John. She was responsible for the nursing in 1,786 auxiliary hospitals and under her guidance 4,730 trained nurses were employed. An additional 762 nurses were trained for service in war hospitals in France and Belgium and 6,666 were despatched to other fronts, making a total of 7,428.

Sarah Swift was awarded the Royal Red Cross (First Class) and also the Order of the British Empire. She was created a Lady of Grace of St. John of Jerusalem and finally in 1919 she was created Dame Grand Cross of the British Empire. In 1916 Dame Sarah Swift was the driving force behind the establishment of the College of Nursing which in 1946 became the Royal College of Nursing with its own Coat-of-Arms and the motto 'Tradismus Lampada' (We hand on the Torch).

Dame Sarah Swift died in London on 27 June 1937 at the age of 83. As a memorial to her the floor of the Lady Chapel in Kirton Parish Church was repaved and a tablet erected together with the illuminated address which had been presented to Dame Sarah by the British Red Cross.

The Swyneford Chantry in Lincoln Cathedral.

Katherine SWYNFORD (1350-1403)

Katherine Swynford was born in 1350 and was the younger daughter of Sir Payne Roelt. In about 1367 she married Sir Hugh Swynford who was in the service of John of Gaunt, Duke of Lancaster. Sir Hugh had manors at Coleby and Kettlethorpe and died in 1372.

Katherine became John of Gaunt's mistress and a member of the household of Mary de Bohun, the wife of Henry of Lancaster. John of Gaunt's second wife died in 1394 and on 13 January 1396 he married Katherine in the Cathedral at Lincoln where she was then living. In the following year their children were declared legitimate except for the succession to the throne.

Katherine died on 10 May 1403 and was buried in Lincoln Cathedral. Through her son John, Katherine was great-great-grandmother of Henry VII, the first of the Tudor Monarchs.

FURTHER READING: Goodman, A. *Katherine Swynford* (Lincoln 1994)

John TAVERNER (*c*1490-1545)

John Taverner appears to have been born in or near Boston in about 1490 but nothing is known of his early life.

In 1524 he was a lay clerk of the choir of the collegiate church of Tattershall. In the autumn of 1525 John Longland, Bishop of Lincoln, invited him to move to Oxford to become instructor of the choristers of the chapel of Cardinal College in Oxford University, which had been recently founded by Cardinal Wolsey. The chapel is now the Cathedral. At first Taverner declined but in 1526 he accepted the post. He was paid £10 a year and given four yards of cloth valued at 3s 4d for livery and 1s 8d a week for commons (food). Taverner is sometimes described as an organist and canon of Cardinal College.

Taverner wrote a considerable number of religious works during his time at Cardinal College and three of these were published by Wynkyn de Worde in 1530. By 1537 he had ended his association with the choir and appears to have returned to Boston. In 1538 he supervised the demolition and burning of the rood screen in St. Botolph's Church.

In 1545 he became an alderman but died soon afterwards and was buried in St. Botolphs.

FURTHER READING: Hand, C. *John Taverner : his life and music* (1978)

Alfred TENNYSON (1809-1892)

The future poet laureate was the fourth of the twelve children of Rev. Dr. George Clayton Tennyson, who was rector of Somersby. Alfred was born on 6 August 1809 and at the age of seven he was sent to live with his grandmother in Louth so that he could attend the Grammar School there. In 1820 he returned to Somersby and remained there until he went to College.

He was an avid reader, especially of poetry, and from an early age he had written 'blank verse in praise of flowers'. In 1827 Alfred and his brother Charles published *Poems by two Brothers*, which contained poems written by Charles between the ages of sixteen and seventeen and by Alfred written between the ages of fifteen and seventeen. They were paid £10 cash and £10 in books and the cash was spent in hiring a carriage which they drove to Mablethorpe.

In February 1828 Alfred Tennyson went up to Trinity College, Cambridge and in June 1829 he won the Chancellor's medal for his verses entitled *Timbuctoo*. In 1830 a volume of poems with the title *Poems chiefly Lyrical* was published. Tennyson left Cambridge in 1831 to return to Somersby without taking a degree, because of his father's ill health. The death of his friend Arthur Hallam in 1833 had a great influence on Tennyson and in later years led to the writing of one of Tennyson's best known poems, *In Memoriam*.

In 1837 the family left Lincolnshire and moved to Epping Forest and in 1840 they moved again, to Tunbridge Wells. Another move was made in 1841, this time to Boxley near Maidstone. In 1842 his *Poems in two volumes* was published and this seems to have established him as the then greatest living poet. In 1845, following a serious illness, he was awarded a pension of £200 per year. In 1850, after a long engagement, Tennyson married Emily Sellwood of Horncastle and in the same year he was appointed Poet Laureate.

In 1853 the Tennysons moved to the Isle of Wight and in 1855 he received a Doctorate in Civil Law from Oxford University. His first meeting with Queen Victoria took place in 1862 and in 1864 the first of his Lincolnshire dialect poems was published with the title *Northern Farmer Old Style*. For the next few years Tennyson devoted himself to his poetry and to travel. In 1873 he was offered a baronetcy which he declined but when the Queen personally offered him a peerage, after much hesitation he accepted.

Alfred Lord Tennyson died on 6 October 1892 and was buried in Westminster Abbey.

FURTHER READING: Martin, R. B. *Tennyson : The Unquiet Heart* (1980)

Margaret Hilda THATCHER (1925-   )

Britain's first woman Prime Minster was born in Grantham on 13 October 1925 and is the daughter of the late Alfred and Beatrice Roberts. Her father kept a grocer's shop and he was a Methodist local preacher and a member of the local council. The family lived above the shop in North Parade.

On 3 September 1930 Margaret Hilda Roberts became a pupil at the local county school and at the age of ten years and six months she won a scholarship to Kesteven and Grantham Girls' School. She became interested in Chemistry and decided to sit the entrance examination for admission to Somerville College, Oxford. Her friend, Margaret Goodrich, the daughter of Canon Goodrich, vicar of Corby Glen, was already an undergraduate at Lady Margaret Hall. If she was to be successful, Margaret needed to learn Latin and her father employed the classics master at the King's School to teach her. She was unsuccessful in the 1942 entrance examination, which she sat in her fourth term in the sixth form, but was accepted in 1943.

From the very beginning Margaret joined the Oxford University Conservative Association and in her last year at Oxford she became the first woman undergraduate to be elected chairman of the Association. At the 1945 general election she canvassed for the Conservatives in Oxford and in Grantham and often spoke to the audiences before the candidate. In

1947, after having graduated with the degree of Bachelor of Science, she started work as a research chemist with the plastics firm British Xylonite at their works in Manningtree, Essex, with a salary of £350 a year. In early 1949 she was adopted as the Conservative candidate for the Dartford constituency, becoming at the age of 23 the youngest woman candidate in the country. Soon after, she moved to the research department of J. Lyons & Company in Hammersmith and obtained lodgings in Dartford. She was defeated at the 1950 election and moved to her own flat in Pimlico but stood again for the same constituency in the 1951 election and was again defeated.

Margaret Roberts had met Denis Thatcher whilst living in Dartford and they married in 1951. She now left full-time employment so that she could study law. In 1953 the twins Carol and Mark were born and in 1954 Mrs. Thatcher was called to the bar. She decided to specialise in tax law and practised for five years until, in 1958, she was adopted as the Conservative candidate for the Finchley constituency. She was elected at the 1959 general election and remained the Member of Parliament for Finchley for the whole of her career in the House of Commons.

In 1961 she was appointed Joint Parliamentary Secretary to the Minister of Pensions and National Insurance and remained there until the defeat of the Conservative Government in 1964. On the election of a Conservative Government in 1970, Margaret Thatcher was appointed Secretary of State for Education and Science, a post she held until the Government was again defeated in 1974. She was elected leader of the Conservative Party in 1975 and when the Conservatives regained power in 1979 she became Prime Minister.

She remained Prime Minister until 1992 and soon after her replacement as leader of the party and Prime Minister she was created a life peer. Her husband, Denis, was created the first baronet Scotney in 1991. Lady Thatcher lists her recreations as music and reading.

FURTHER READING: Young, H. *One of us: a biography of Margaret Thatcher* (1989)

Sybil THORNDIKE (1882-1976)

Dame Sybil Thorndike was born in Gainsborough on 24 October 1882 and was the eldest of the four children of Rev. Arthur Thorndike and his wife Agnes Bowers. Her father was appointed a minor canon of Rochester Cathedral before Sybil was two years old and the family left Lincolnshire.

Sybil and her brother Russell from a very early age showed great interest in amateur dramatics and by the age of four Sybil performed at family gatherings. By the age of seven they had written and performed their own play entitled *The Dentist's Chair* which had the sub-title *Saw their silly heads off!* When Russell went away to school Sybil turned from acting to the piano, which she played at Sunday School. At the age of eleven she played Beethoven at a London Concert but the theatre was not altogether forgotten. Sybil still performed in plays at her school and was in demand for local amateur productions.

Her parents expected her to make a career as a concert pianist but a painful left wrist ruled this out and she auditioned unsuccessfully as a singer. Finally in 1903 Sybil and Russell auditioned for admission to 'Ben Greet's Academy', which had been founded as an acting school in 1896. Sybil's parents agreed that she should join the Greet Company on an American tour in 1904 and thus her early acting career was established.

Full details of the numerous plays, films and television productions are recorded in Sheridan Morley's biography. Clearly Dame Sybil's Lincolnshire roots can have had little if any influence on her but it is interesting to note that one of this country's greatest actresses was born in the county.

Dame Sybil Thorndike died on 9 June 1976.

FURTHER READING: Morley, Sheridan. *Sybil Thorndike: A Life in the Theatre* (1977)

William TRITTON (1875-1946)

William Tritton was born in Islington on 19 June 1875 and was the son of a stockbroker. He was educated at Christ's College, Finchley and King's College, London.

Tritton commenced his working life with a firm of hydraulic engineers and became an inspector of steel rails before joining a Chiswick firm responsible for making circulating pumps for installation in torpedo boats. Tritton worked for a time with the Metropolitan Electric Supply Company and the Linotype Company Ltd. This involved him in considerable continental travel.

In 1905 he became General Manager of William Foster & Co. Ltd. of Lincoln and it was his energy and ability which enabled the firm to prosper. William Tritton came to prominence through the part he played in the design and production of the tank which greatly assisted the victory of the allies in the First World War. He had been asked to discuss the problem of transporting fifteen-inch howitzers and his proposals, together with those of Rear Admiral Sir Richard Bacon, were put to Winston Churchill. This resulted in an order which was placed with Tritton's firm. The resulting trials led to Churchill asking if a machine could be developed capable of crossing trenches and so the tank came into being.

After several earlier models had been discarded the tank was first used in action in France on 15 September 1916. William Tritton was knighted in 1917 and appointed Director of Construction in the Mechanical Warfare Supply Department. Sir William played little part in public life but became a Justice of the Peace in 1934. He died in Lincoln on 24 September 1946.

Richard TURPIN (1706-1739)

Dick Turpin, the famous highwayman, was born at Hempstead near Saffron Walden in 1705 or 1706 and most of his criminal activities were confined to Essex and the London area. In May 1737 he murdered a man in Epping Forest, after which he moved first to Brough on the north bank of the Humber and later to Welton, both of which are near the traditional site of the ancient ferry over the Humber. He selected Long Sutton as his southern base, as this gave him easy access to Norfolk and Cambridgeshire. It also meant that any horses which disappeared in the Long Sutton area could be disposed of without question in Yorkshire.

Turpin used the name John Palmer at this time and his first recorded crime in Lincolnshire seems to have been the theft of a brown gelding from Charles Townsend, the Curate of Pinchbeck, in 1738. He left the horse with his father, John Turpin, who kept the Bell Inn, at Hempstead in Essex. Not surprisingly the acquisition of a new horse created some comment in the village and on 12 September 1738 John Turpin was charged with stealing the horse. He protested that the horse had been left by his son. In the meantime a warrant had been issued for the arrest of Dick Turpin for sheep stealing but he escaped to Yorkshire, stealing on the way three horses belonging to Thomas Creasey of Heckington. On 2 October he was arrested for disorderly behaviour in Brough and he was committed to the House of Correction in Beverley, riding there on one of the horses stolen from Heckington!

Enquiries revealed that he was in the habit of travelling into Lincolnshire, returning with plenty of money and several horses. Turpin said that he had lived for two years in Long Sutton with his father and sister and was a butcher. The magistrates made enquiries of their colleagues in Long Sutton and they replied that Palmer's father did not live in Long Sutton but Palmer himself had lived there for a short period and was wanted in connection with horse stealing. As a result, Turpin alias Palmer was sent under guard to York Castle. By chance a neighbour of Thomas Creasey's, one John Baxter, stayed overnight at Brough, where he saw a mare and foal like those stolen at Heckington. On his return to Heckington he reported this to Creasey. As a result, Turpin was eventually identified and he was tried at York Assizes on 19 March 1739, the chief witness being Thomas Creasey. He was sentenced to death and executed at York on Saturday 7 April 1739.

John TWIGG (1887-1960)

John Twigg was born at Maltby-le-Marsh and he was educated at Alford Grammar School. The family moved to Tothby Manor near Alford in 1915 and when his father died in 1921 John took over the tenancy of the farm. He and his wife Mollie remained at Tothby until John retired in 1940 to live in East Street, Alford.

John Twigg was an incorrigible practical joker and the first recorded incident was when an open grave appeared on a green lane near Maltby-le-Marsh. John arranged for two residents who were conducting a long standing feud to meet at the spot. He said that the grave had been dug by gypsies and what took place when the two astonished men saw it is not recorded.

When John and one of the antagonists became next door neighbours in Alford they also became close friends but even so the whole incident was blamed on John! At the turn of the century at five o'clock one June morning the inhabitants of Maltby were woken by the brass band striking up *Abide with me*. Rumour soon spread throughout the village that John Twigg was going to shoot himself. Soon a large crowd gathered including the parson and undertaker. John placed a U-shaped tube to his chest and fired a pistol into the other end. He survived and the undertaker complained that he had wasted his time.

John did not get on very well with the parson, so he forged a letter to the parson from the local blacksmith, who was well-known as an atheist, and another from the parson to the blacksmith. Not surprisingly there was quite a set-to between the parson and the blacksmith and in the end the blacksmith put a notice in his shop apologising for something he hadn't done!

John Twigg in the stocks at Alford, 1958.

There was no malice in John. He was really simply bubbling over with a love of life. He once said that his recreations were shooting ash off cigarettes whilst they were still in the smoker's mouth with a target pistol and standing on his head on house ridges and chimney tops. He might have added 'debunking the pompous and making the most of opportunities'.

John and his wife Mollie had five sons and soon after the youngest, David, was born, John was seen walking along Tothby Lane to Alford pushing a pram. When John was asked to display the new arrival a piglet appeared from under the covers! The boys kept pet mice and these soon began to multiply at a prodigious rate. John advertised in the local press 'TWIGG'S MOUSE FARM - any quantity supplied' and was surprised to receive an order from Billy Butlin to supply 3000 mice to the Holiday Camp at Ingoldmells. John's son Tom remembers travelling with his brothers in the car to Butlin's, with sample boxes of mice on their knees!

John was somewhat infamous for his pets - the most notorious being a wolf! This usually vicious animal was devoted to him and he would take it for walks. On one notable market Day he took the wolf to the Windmill Bar at Alford. The wolf died in the early 1930s and is buried in the shrubbery at Tothby Manor, with a tombstone on which is inscribed: 'Here lies Sally pet wolf / A better creature than you or I'

Even in his seventies, John continued with his hobby of standing on his head on any conceivable occasion. When a building was being demolished in the South Market Place at Alford, which is across the road from the Windmill Hotel, a slightly inebriated customer on leaving the bar was amazed to see John standing on his hands on the ridge. The poor man swore not to touch another drop! One fine summer in the mid-thirties the neighbouring farmers had cut their hay but John left one of the Park Lane meadows uncut. When asked about it, he said he couldn't cut it until the following week. When the *Lincolnshire Standard* appeared at the week-end the following advertisement appeared: 'John Twigg of Tothby apologises to the courting couples of Alford. He cannot delay cutting the hay any longer'.

John Twigg became internationally famous in 1934 when he dropped an egg from an aircraft. At that time a trip by air was a novelty and John decided that he ought to try the experience and took advantage of a 'five bob round the town' trip starting at Miles Cross Hill. The pilot obligingly flew low over Alford. John just happened to have a bad egg wrapped in a newspaper in his pocket and this landed on the roof of the Police House, which was adjacent to the Police Station. He was summoned to appear at Alford Magistrates' Court, charged with 'dropping a certain object from an aircraft flying' and this was the first such case ever brought under the Air Navigation Act.

At the hearing, John asserted that he was aiming at the Saturday afternoon shoppers in the Market Place or at the Bowling Green which are, by air, only a few seconds from the Police Station, which was then in Park Lane and it might be that an inexperienced bomb aimer could mistake his target! S. B. Carnley, for the defence, asked the magistrates to ignore 'fantastic statements which had appeared in certain sections of the press alleging that a dangerous missile had been dropped'. Major Rawnsley, Chairman of the Bench, remarked on the danger and the foolishness of John's escapade before fining him two pounds with fifteen shillings costs! There were many more such incidents but space does not permit me to record them here.

On 9 August 1958 the following three 'charges' were brought against John Twigg: 1. Harbouring on his person certain wild animals and reptiles of a ferocious nature with intent to surreptitiously release the same amongst the inhabitants for the purpose of creating 'breeze' and panic. 2. Writing and exhibiting certain prose and verse to the detriment of the users of the highway adjoining his premises. 3. Throwing eggs of uncertain age or vintage at the abode of the constable of the parish.

A plaque recording these charges was placed in the Council Chamber at Alford and this also records that, 'Being found guilty he was forcibly and unceremoniously confined to the stocks until his fealty was respited'. This confirms the affection with which John was held even by those whom he must have plagued at times. How John Twigg managed to survive apparently without accident is a mystery but he died in May 1960 at the age of 73.

James Ward USHER (1845-1921)

James Ward Usher was born on 1 January 1845 in a house on Lincoln High Street, the site of which is now occupied by Barclays Bank. He joined his father in their jewellery and watchmaking business after completing his education at Lincoln School and Totteridge Park School in Hertfordshire. The shop was opposite the house in the High Street, facing the Cornhill and Usher was the first person to introduce electricity into business premises in the City. This he did, in 1886, by installing his own generating plant.

A visit to the Sale Rooms of Christies in London in March 1883 inspired Usher to collect objects of beauty. By 1911 his collection had reached its peak, having been acquired by travelling many thousands of miles. In 1916 he published *An Art Collector's Treasures,* describing some eighty items from his collection which he illustrated in colour. Before he began compiling his book he decided to appoint a manager and as a result a young man was summoned by telegram for interview. He duly arrived at 2 pm on the appointed day but on calling at the shop in High Street was told Mr. Usher would not be available until 6.30 pm. When the young E. A. Taylor called back for his interview, Usher spent the whole time talking about his collection and when he left at about 1.30 am Taylor didn't know if he had the job! He returned next morning and was engaged as manager, which post he filled for many years.

It was James Ward Usher who first popularised the Lincoln Imp as a memento for visitors to Lincoln. He patented the idea and for many years produced tie pins and brooches depicting Lincoln's mascot.

Usher died in 1921 leaving his collection to the City of Lincoln and sufficient money to establish the Usher Art Gallery on Lindum Hill. The building, to the design of Sir Reginald Blomfield, R.A., was opened by the then Prince of Wales (later King Edward VIII and Duke of Windsor) in May 1927. Items bequeathed by Usher included porcelain, enamels, portrait miniatures, watches of the sixteenth, seventeenth and eighteenth centuries, silver and a signed portrait of himself in the robes of the Sherriff of Lincoln.

Edward Chad VARAH (1911-   )

Chad Varah was born in the Vicarage at Barton-on-Humber on 12 November 1911, the eldest son of Canon and Mrs. W. E. Varah. He was named after the founder of the eighth century St. Peter's Church at Barton, St. Chad, and his surname is found on Yorkshire tombstones as far back as 1490.

Chad was educated at Worksop College and Keble College, Oxford where he read Natural Sciences and received his B. A. in 1933. An adopted uncle who was a retired missionary Bishop persuaded him to become a student at Lincoln Theological College, where his theological training was conducted under Michael Ramsey, later Archbishop of Canterbury.

In 1935 Chad Varah was made deacon to serve in the newly created parish of St. Giles in Lincoln, and the following year he had the unique distinction of being ordained Priest in the recently consecrated Church of St.Giles with the well beloved Canon Daniels as vicar. Owing to the illness of the vicar, his first task after ordination was to conduct the funeral service of a fourteen year old girl who had committed suicide through ignorance of the sexual problems of puberty and having no one to whom she could talk. This led Chad Varah to give talks on sex to the young, first at St Giles Youth Club and then to couples about to be married. In 1938 he moved first to Putney and two years later to Barrow-in-Furness and then on in 1942 to Holy Trinity, Blackburn as vicar. In 1950 he moved back to London, to St. Paul's Clapham Junction, where, in addition to his parish work he was script writer for the teenage magazines *Eagle* and *Girl*.

Then in 1953 Chad was offered the living of the Lord Mayor's parish church of St. Stephen, Walbrook. As this parish has few resident parishioners, he had the opportunity he had been looking for — to found a service for the suicidal which he called The Samaritans. So the work began for which Chad Varah had dedicated himself in 1935 at St. Giles. When he first announced that people contemplating suicide were invited to telephone him on Man 9000, he had no idea that he was founding a worldwide movement.

In 1940 Chad Varah had married Doris Susan Whanslawe (who died in 1993) and they had a daughter and four sons (three of them triplets). Chad Varah was awarded the O. B. E. in 1969 and was made a Prebendary of St. Paul's Cathedral in 1975. He has received a number of other honours including an honorary Doctorate of Law from Leicester University. On the rare occasions when he has any spare time he likes travelling off the beaten track and reading. His autobiography was published in 1992 and in October 1993 he unveiled a plaque at Lincoln Theological College commemorating his time there and the commencement of his ministry at St. Giles.

FURTHER READING: Varah, Chad. *Before I Die Again* (1992)

HEREWARD the Wake (*c*1070)

It appears that Hereward was the son of Leofric of Bourn, but this legendary source is somewhat suspect. However, it seems reasonably certain that Hereward was a Lincolnshire man and *Domesday Book* shows that he held land in several places in Lincolnshire.

Hereward was apparently banished from England because of his violence but returned to England to oppose the Normans. In 1070 he joined the Danes and attacked Peterborough Abbey, burning both monastery and town. From Peterborough, Hereward and his men went to Ely where the Danes left with their loot, leaving Hereward to resist the Normans. This they did with great success and Ely became a refuge for those who would not accept Norman rule. For some time they resisted the might of the Norman army but eventually Hereward was forced to retreat with as many of his men as could escape. At this point little authentic history is recorded but many legends arose and Hereward is said to have been pardoned by William the Conqueror and died in peace. The title 'the Wake' was given to Hereward by John of Peterborough and means 'the watchful one'.

FURTHER READING: *Domesday Book*; *The Anglo-Saxon Chronicle*; *Florence of Worcester*; Kingsley, Charles. *Hereward the Wake*

William WATKINS (1834-1926)

William Watkins was born in 1834 at Leylands Farm, Droitwich. In 1854 he became an articled pupil with Henry Day, who was architect to the Dean and Chapter of Worcester Cathedral. After he had completed the five years required by the articles he remained with Henry Day as an assistant architect. Watkins left in October 1858 and after six months in Leicester joined Henry Goddard of Lincoln. It is not clear if the six months in Leicester were actually spent in Goddards branch office in that town.

On 20 February 1867 Watkins married Kate Devereux Garnham of Beccles and they lived in a house on Steep Hill, Lincoln. In 1877 he built a house which was called Leyland House in The Grove, Lincoln. He entered seven open competitions, five of which he won and thus laid the foundations upon which his architectural career was built. The winning designs were for Brigg Methodist Church which was built in 1865, Grantham Town Hall (1867-9), Doncaster Corn Exchange (1870), Kidderminster Work House and an Orphanage in Worcester.

In 1880 William Watkins formed a partnership with William Scorer and the firm designed a wide range of buildings both in the city and county, which included banks, schools, commercial buildings, hospitals, churches and some important houses. Watkins was responsible for the restoration of the buildings on the High Bridge, in Lincoln and the Greyfriars north of St. Swithin's Church.

William Watkins was elected a Fellow of the Royal Institute of British Architects in 1881. From 1900 onwards he published a number of papers and reports on archaeology and antiquarian features of Lincoln. Watkins was elected a member of the City Council and was

Mayor in 1888-9. He was appointed a Justice of the Peace on 8 April 1901. William Watkins retired in 1918 and handed over the business to his son William Gregory Watkins and died on 26 April 1926.

FURTHER READING: Burgess, Sybil *et al.*, *The Victorian Façade* (1990)

William WAYNFLETE (*c*1395-1486)

William Waynflete was born as William Patten in Wainfleet in the late fourteenth or early fifteenth century. His father was Richard Patten alias Barbour of gentry stock and his mother was Margaret Brereton whose family held the manor of Dalby.

William was educated at Winchester College and, apparently, New College, Oxford and was ordained in Spalding parish church on 21 April 1420. Soon after Eton College was founded by Henry VI, William Waynflete was appointed its provost and in 1447 he was appointed Bishop of Winchester. Bishop Waynflete founded Magdalen College, Oxford in 1448 for the study of theology and philosophy. On 11 October 1456 the Bishop was appointed Lord Chancellor of England.

Although most of William Waynflete's career was spent in southern England, he maintained close links with his native county. His career was dominated by his interest in education and he played a leading role in some of the changes which transformed education in fifteenth century England. Bishop Waynflete died on 11 August 1486 and was buried in Winchester Cathedral.

FURTHER READING: Davis, Virginia. *William Waynflete: Bishop and Educationalist* (Woodbridge, 1994)

Augustine WEBSTER (died 1535)

After studying at Cambridge Augustine Webster became a Carthusian monk and in 1531 prior of the Charterhouse at Axholme. While on a visit to the London Charterhouse he accompanied John Houghton and Robert Lawrence to a meeting with Thomas Cromwell in an attempt to amend the wording of the Oath of Supremacy, in order to make it acceptable to those who could not agree to the assumption by King Henry VIII of the title Supreme Head of the Church. This was refused and they were convicted of treason and executed at Tyburn on 4 May 1535. All three were canonised by Pope Paul VI on 15 October 1970.

Charles WESLEY (1708-1788)

Charles Wesley was born at Epworth in 1708 and he was not expected to survive his premature birth. His early education, like all the Wesley children, was by his mother and he was sent to Westminster School at the age of nine. He became a King's Scholar and captain of the school before going up to Christ Church, Oxford.

Charles had an inquisitive mind and seemed to his brother John to pay too much attention to the worldly social life of the University. However, Charles gathered round him a circle of undergraduates for prayer and bible study which became known as the Holy Club. John Wesley gave strong support to the Holy Club and the prayer meetings and discussions became strictly regulated, with rules and plans for each day's activities. It was the methodical planning of their activities which gave the nickname 'Methodists' to the members of the group. Charles was ordained and appointed to lecture at Christ Church but when his brother John joined General Oglethorpe's expedition to America Charles was persuaded to accompany the party as the General's Secretary.

The brothers soon returned to England and Charles resumed his preaching in both Oxford and London, eventually travelling further afield and preaching in the open air. It was during his travels about England and Wales that he wrote many of the hymns which are so familiar to us. In 1749 Charles married Sally Gwynne, the daughter of a wealthy Welsh squire and magistrate who was also a devoted churchman. Poor health and infirmity curtailed his travels and he moved to London in 1771. He devoted his time to preaching twice each Sunday at the City Road Chapel, prison visiting, hymn writing and to his family.

It is, of course, for his hymn writing that Charles Wesley is best remembered. Such favourites as *Jesu, lover of my soul; Soldiers of Christ arise; Oh for a thousand tongues to sing; Love divine all loves excelling* and *Gentle Jesus, meek and mild,* with many more, came from his pen.

Charles Wesley died in his eightieth year and was buried in Marylebone.

FURTHER READING: Gill, F. C. *Charles Wesley: the first Methodist* (1964)

John WESLEY (1703-1791)

John Wesley was the second son to survive childhood of the nineteen children born to Samuel Wesley, the incumbent of Epworth. John's elder brother Samuel had been born twelve years earlier and his younger brother Charles was born four years later. John's early years were spent mostly in the company of his five sisters and his mother, Susannah, who had a special attachment to him. She wrote of John 'I intend to be more particularly careful of the soul of this child than ever I have been'.

John's father Samuel was a man of strong views on morality and religion. He was fearless in expressing his opinions regardless of the consequences. He was also a scholar and this had a strong influence on his children and his wife, who was a gifted and methodical woman. Both parents had a puritan background but had reverted at an early age to strict Anglicanism. In February 1709, Samuel Wesley's hostile and ignorant parishioners set fire to the vicarage, which was gutted. The father rescued the children and nurse, who brought Charles to safety. It was then realised that John was still asleep in the house but he was awakened by the noise of the burning thatch. He managed to break a window and climb out just before the roof fell in. This childhood experience had a lasting effect on John, who appears to have regarded his deliverance as the hand of God choosing him for a great purpose.

At the age of 10½, John went for six years as a foundation scholar to Charterhouse School in London, which had been founded 100 years earlier by the will of Sir Thomas Sutton of Knaith Hall in Lincolnshire. He declared later in life that his robust constitution and endurance were due partly to the frugal fare of his school days!

In 1716 Epworth Rectory was plagued by hauntings. These manifestations consisted of strange knockings, rattlings and footsteps up and down the stairs. In 1717 the bed on which John's sister Nancy was sitting was lifted in the air several times before the eyes of her sisters and the manservant. Their father, who had rebuked the family for believing in such things, was himself pushed violently against the door of his study. The family became accustomed to the 'ghost', whom they called 'Old Jeffrey'. There were many other authenticated phenomena which could not be accounted for by any natural causes, and the mystery was never solved.

At the age of seventeen John left school and entered Christ Church College, Oxford. Although he had a scholarship worth £40 from Charterhouse he was always short of money since his father was continually in debt at home. He was unable to afford a wig, which was the fashion, and wore his hair long to save the expense of a barber. At Oxford he kept a diary written in code consisting of Greek, English and Hebrew letters, numbers, dots and dashes! He graduated B.A. in 1724 and M.A. a year later. In March 1726 Wesley was made a Fellow of Lincoln College, which had been founded 300 years earlier by the Bishop of Lincoln to train men for the Church. In April 1726 he walked the 150 miles to his home in Epworth partly because he enjoyed walking but also because it was more economical.

For two years he assisted his father in his parish but in November 1729 he returned to Lincoln College as tutor in the Classics, Divinity and Logic. As a result of reading Thomas à Kempis's book *On the Imitation of Christ* and Taylor's *Holy Living* and *Holy Dying* he 'set in earnest upon a new life'. His younger brother Charles was the centre of a small group known as the Holy Club, which was devoted to studying the New Testament and ways in which they could become better Christians. The group grew and came to be called the Methodists, because of the set of rules or methods to which they endeavoured to bind themselves.

In 1735, the year of his father's death, John sailed to America as a missionary to the Indians of Georgia and as Chaplain to the people of Savannah. He persuaded his brother Charles to join him and to act as Secretary to General Oglethorpe, who had founded the colony in 1732. Unfortunately, John did not succeed as a missionary and he returned to England in 1737 in a rather depressed frame of mind. On 24 May 1738 he attended a meeting in London and he records in his Journal that 'I felt my heart strangely warmed'. It was from that moment that John dated his real conversion and the beginning of a new outlook on life.

Because the churches were closed to them John and his fellow Methodists preached in the open fields to large audiences. Even at Epworth, his birthplace, the curate would not let him in the church and he stood on his father's tomb to preach. An old building at Moorfields became the London headquarters and other permanent meeting places were set up in Bristol and Newcastle-on-Tyne. John travelled far and wide preaching often against organised heckling and even threats of physical violence. A great supporter of the Methodists was Robert Carr Brackenbury of Raithby near Spilsby and a loft over a stable at Raithby Hall was converted for use as a chapel. John was careful to preach only at times which would not interfere with the service times at the parish church and used language which all could understand.

In 1788 Charles Wesley died and John himself died three years later in his 88th year.

FURTHER READING: Pollock, J. *John Wesley* (1989)

John WHITGIFT (?1530-1604)

Archbishop John Whitgift was born at Grimsby in about 1530 and was the eldest son of a wealthy merchant. His uncle Robert Whitgift was abbot of nearby Wellow, an Augustinian monastery and took an interest in John's early education. On his advice, John was sent to St. Anthony's School in London. He went up to Queen's College, Cambridge but soon transferred to Pembroke Hall where he came under the influence of the Master, Nicholas Ridley. Whitgift graduated with the degree of Bachelor of Arts in 1553 and was awarded his Master's Degree in 1557.

On 31 May 1555 Whitgift was elected to a fellowship and took Holy Orders in 1560. His first sermon was preached in the University Church of Great St. Mary's and in the same year Whitgift was invited to become Chaplain to the Bishop of Ely. In 1563, he was awarded the degree of Bachelor of Divinity and was also appointed Lady Margaret Professor of Divinity. On 6 April 1567 Whitgift was elected to the mastership of Pembroke Hall and awarded a Doctorate in Divinity on 4 July 1567. He became Master of Trinity College, a Canon of Ely and, in 1571, he was elected Dean of Lincoln Cathedral. In 1572 he became Rector of Laceby and was Vice-Chancellor of Cambridge University in 1570 and 1573. In 1576 John Whitgift became Bishop of Worcester and finally in 1583 Archbishop of Canterbury.

Whitgift was often invited to preach before Queen Elizabeth I, who came to regard him as her confessor. The Queen was frequently his guest at his London home, Lambeth Palace, and perhaps his popularity with the Queen accounts, to some extent, for his rapid promotion.

When Whitgift's father died he left him a considerable fortune and he was able to restore much of the pre-Reformation magnificence of the primacy. He also built almshouses and a free school at Croydon.

Archbishop Whitgift was a staunch Protestant and in 1583 he prohibited all preaching in private houses. He decreed that no one was to conduct services or preach unless they had subscribed to the Royal Supremacy, abided by the *Book of Common Prayer* and accepted the Thirty-Nine Articles. Archbishop Whitgift died on 29 February 1604 and was buried in St. Nicholas Church, Croydon.

FURTHER READING: Brook, V. J. K. *Whitgift and the English Church* (1964)

Francis WILLIS (1718-1807)

Francis Willis was born on 17 August 1718 and was the third of the four sons of Canon John Willis, a prebendary of Lincoln Cathedral. At the age of fifteen he entered Lincoln College, Oxford, gaining his BA on 21 March 1738 and his MA two years later. Francis became a Fellow and later vice-principal of Brasenose College. He took Holy Orders but had a strong inclination to the study of medicine and even whilst an undergraduate he studied medicine and attended lectures in that subject.

Willis commenced his ministry as Rector of St. John's, Wapping but returned to Lincolnshire in 1745 to become vicar of Ashby de la Launde. Four years later he married Mary Curtois, youngest daughter of the Rev. John Curtois, of Branston and they had five sons.

Francis Willis is said to have first practised medicine without a licence, but in 1759 Oxford University conferred on him the degrees of MB and MD. He was a member of the committee which established Lincoln County Hospital in 1768 and a year later was appointed Physician. Dr. Willis treated successfully a number of cases of mental illness and patients were brought to him from great distances. He bought Greatford Hall near Stamford which became the first of his two private homes for the care of the mentally ill. He became highly regarded for his treatment of a malady the cause of which was little understood at that time.

For some time the health of King George III had been causing his doctors considerable anxiety and by 1780 it had become obvious that he was suffering another mental breakdown similar to the first in 1765. This time the King became very violent and, in November 1788, Francis Willis was called in. However, he encountered considerable opposition from the King's regular physicians, being 'considered by some not much better than a mountebank and not far different from some that are confined in his house'. Dr. Willis considered that the patient should be gently dealt with and allowed greater freedom. This approach was far in advance of his time and encountered much opposition from those who advocated restraint. However, Willis became extremely popular at Court and was described as 'a man in ten thousand; open, honest, dauntless, light-hearted, innocent and high minded' and 'the very image of simplicity, quite a good, plain, old-fashioned country parson'. By February 1789 the King began to respond to Willis's treatment and his doctors reported a remarkable improvement in His Majesty's health.

Soon Willis was able to return to Greatford and his practice but his reputation was much enhanced and his aid was sought by the Queen of Portugal, who was 'seriously disturbed'. Under Dr. Willis's care she was able to regain her health and as a mark of her gratitude she gave him £20,000! Dr Willis's practice grew and he opened a second treatment centre at Shillingthorpe Hall in the adjoining parish of Braceborough to house fifteen patients. Francis Willis died on 5 December 1807 at the age of 89 and was buried at Greatford where his sons erected a monument to his memory.

John Willis, the second son, became a doctor and assisted his father during the King's first illness and attended him during his subsequent bouts. He took over the running of Shillingthorpe Hall and Greatford House as his father became more infirm. His youngest brother, Robert Darling Willis, MD was appointed physician-in-ordinary to the King before the Monarch's last illness, which began in 1811 and ended with his death in 1820.

Edward James WILSON (died 1854)

Edward James Wilson developed his lifelong interest in the history, antiquities and ancient buildings of Lincolnshire from early childhood. As a schoolboy, he was so fascinated by books that he climbed the walls of the Wren Library of the Cathedral and entered through an open window. On leaving school he worked for his father, who was a carpenter and joiner at the Cathedral and it was here that he became a skilled wood carver.

In 1811 he undertook the restoration of the intricate wooden ceiling of the Longland chantry. His strong Roman Catholic faith was inherited from his mother. Wilson collaborated with A. C. Pugin, an aristocratic refugee from the French Revolution who was a skilled draughtsman and father of the famous architect, in the production in 1821-5 of *Specimens of Gothic Architecture* and in 1831-6 of *Examples of Gothic Architecture*. Pugin produced the drawings and Wilson the text, much of which related to Lincoln. Wilson also compiled a *Glossary of Technical Terms,* which was a pioneering work in the field of architecture. For some thirty years up to 1835 Wilson collaborated with John Britton in several series of popular topographical works which gave the 'man in the street' an insight into Wilson's speciality, Gothic architecture, and stimulated an interest in local history. At a time when many medieval Lincolnshire buildings were threatened with demolition or unsympathetic restoration, Wilson was able to influence their preservation. As County Surveyor from 1835 to 1845 he restored the keep, gates and walls of Lincoln Castle which were in danger of falling into ruin.

Wilson's first task as an architect was the reconstruction of Messingham church in 1817-18. Welton-by-Lincoln church was rebuilt under Wilson's direction in 1823-24, Haxey was restored in 1825-26, new roofs and porch were constructed at Louth in 1825-27, the tower at West Rasen was rebuilt in 1828/9 and much other work on parish churches and the Cathedral was undertaken under Wilson's direction. He also built domestic and farm buildings and his work extended beyond his native county into Nottinghamshire and Leicestershire. Wilson served the City of Lincoln as a Lighting and Paving Commissioner in 1831 and in 1832 he was a member of a committee set up to propose street names. He became a magistrate in 1836 and an alderman in 1838 becoming Mayor in 1851/2.

As an antiquary, Wilson compiled a considerable collection of papers relating to the architecture, archaeology, topography and indeed every aspect of the history of the city and county. The collection includes invaluable drawings of buildings which no longer exist. This collection of drawings was no doubt influenced by his employment in 1828 by the Lighting and Paving Commissioners to make a survey and valuation of all rateable property in the city. He also collected material relating to the county, parish by parish. including notes on family history and archaeological finds. Unfortunately, after Wilson died on 8 September 1854 his manuscript collections and library were dispersed and much has not survived. Fortunately a large part of the collections was purchased by the Society of Antiquaries in 1901 and microfilm copies are available in the Lincolnshire Archives Office.

In recent years the tombstone in Hainton churchyard commemorating Edward James Wilson and his wife Mary was restored as the result of an appeal for funds by the Society for Lincolnshire History and Archaeology.

Henry WINN (1816-1914)

Henry Winn was born at Fulletby near Horncastle on 23 January 1816 and he was the eldest child of a shoemaker. His father died when Henry was ten years old, leaving his mother with six children. Henry was forced to leave Belchford Day School to help run the family business.

When he was 24 years old he married Maria Maltby of Belchford and during their 29 year marriage Maria bore 21 children but only four survived. His mother having remarried, Henry and Maria lived in the family house and continued to run the shoemaking business. Only two years, later they both became seriously ill and the business had to close down. Henry had never really taken to shoemaking and after recovering he became the village grocer. He also turned his hand to paper hanging, acted as auctioneer's clerk, taught himself land surveying and was overseer, assessor and collector of taxes!

In 1845 he became the Parish Clerk for Fulletby at a salary of two guineas a year. This was a post he had actually held since the age of fourteen because the officially elected Clerk could neither read nor write! Henry continued in office until 1910 when he retired at the age of 94 after over 80 years service. Winn was sworn in as Constable for Fulletby in 1845 and, in 1850, when the village school was built, Henry and his wife became teachers.

Despite all his interests he still found time for community work and was member and secretary of several village societies. He was a particularly keen worker for the temperance movement. His very full life did not prevent him from travelling extensively around the county and he recorded his experiences in journals and in verse. All his correspondence was recorded in notebooks as were his thoughts on many subjects including his family, the scenery and local history. Many of his articles appeared in local newspapers and these were on such diverse subjects as Celebrities, Monuments, Place Names, Curiosities and, indeed, almost every subject connected with Lincolnshire.

Henry Winn was a remarkable man especially when it is remembered that his only education was at Fulletby Sunday School and, to the age of eleven, at the Day School in the neighbouring village of Belchford. He was over 90 when he collected all his notes on Fulletby together into two volumes which he placed in the Parish Chest. On 17 October 1914 in his ninety-third year this true Lincolnshire personality died. Unfortunately his papers were widely scattered and some were eventually sold at Sotheby's. Fortunately some of his papers survive in the Lincolnshire Archives Office and Lincoln Central Library and these confirm his remarkable versatility.

FURTHER READING: Baker, Mrs. F. L. *Poems of Henry Winn* (1965); Burton, Mrs. J. *Henry Winn - The Man of Words* (1984)

Peter de WINT (1784-1849)

Peter de Wint was born on 21 January 1784 at Henley, Staffordshire and was the fourth child of Dr. Henry de Wint, a Dutchman who had trained as a doctor in London. It was intended that Peter should follow his father into the medical profession but in 1802 he was apprenticed to the engraver and portrait painter, John Raphael Smith. Smith realised that Peter was a gifted landscape painter and allowed him to cancel his indentures in 1806, provided he gave him eighteen of his oil paintings over the following two years!

It was at this time that de Wint met William Hilton (q.v.) who came from Lincoln and they became lifelong friends. They set up house together in Broad Street, Golden Square, London intending to earn their living from painting. Peter de Wint married Hilton's sister Harriet in 1810 and they continued to live together until Hilton was appointed keeper of the Royal Academy in 1827, when he moved to Somerset House. It was on a visit to the family home of the Hiltons in Lincoln in 1806 that de Wint first met his future wife and it was also on this visit that he developed his love of river scenery and the flatlands which, in his paintings, he covered with cattle.

Peter de Wint's most regular patron appears to have been Richard Ellison of Sudbrooke Holme near Lincoln. It is his paintings of Lincoln and the surrounding countryside for which de Wint is best remembered, although he also found subjects in Yorkshire, the Lake District and in Wales. In 1814 de Wint bought the Hilton's family home on Motherby Hill together with a piece of land in Union Road near the castle walls for £1,175 and planned to retire there. However, during a visit to Wales in 1833 he caught a cold which developed into bronchitis, from which he suffered for the remainder of his life. He was advised to remain in London and the Lincoln house was let and sold in 1846. Peter de Wint died in 1849.

Margaret WINTRINGHAM (1879-1955)

Margaret Longbottom married Thomas Wintringham of Little Grimsby Hall in 1903. She was a native of Keighley and had been educated at the Girls' Grammar School in that town. After her marriage she became a headmistress in Grimsby. Her husband became the independent Liberal Member of Parliament for Louth and when he died in 1921 his widow Margaret decided to stand at the by-election.

In deference to her husband's memory she did not canvass but still won the seat and thus became the first native-born woman Member of Parliament. She was very popular and increased her majority at the election in 1923 but was defeated at the election in October 1924. Mrs Wintringham contested the Louth seat again in 1929 and the Anglesey seat in 1935 but was unsuccessful on both occasions.

During the first World War Margaret Wintringham served in the Voluntary Aid Detachment. She also chaired the Women's War Agricultural Committee. After the war she remained in public service as a magistrate and also served on the Grimsby Education Committee and Lincolnshire Agricultural Committee. She represented Caistor on Lindsey County Council from 1933 until 1945 and died on 10 March 1955.

INDEX

People with main subject entries in the book are given in **Bold** type. Publications, dramatic and musical works, works of art and newspapers are given entirely in *italics*. Ships are given in *italics*, with the definite article or 'HMS' in roman. Towns and place names outside Lincolnshire include in most cases the relevant present day county or country, except where the place is so well-known for this to be self-evident. Places within the historic (pre-1974) county of Lincolnshire are given without the county.

Square brackets [ ] in entries regarding people denote either differing popular forms of their name when the subject is indexed under their given name and not the one they were generally known by, or, where specifically indicated, aliases. Square brackets in entries regarding places or institutions give alternative or former names, not necessarily indexed elsewhere. Square brackets in entries regarding publications, dramatic and musical works and works of art give the name of the author where appropriate. The definite article has been disregarded, and rather than index *all* the differing forms of what is now the present-day USA, this has been indexed as 'America', throughout.

To prevent needless repetition, the details of publications given in the 'further reading' entries after each subject in the main text have not been re-indexed here.

LIST OF SUBSCRIBERS

John R Anthony
Anthea Ashmore
David Ian Asman Esq
Alfred John Atkinson
Richard Austin-Cooper FCIB FRSA
Isabel Bailey
Coun The Revd Bill Baker
E Ballard
John L Barber
Philip Barnatt
Elizabeth A Barrick
Mrs Maple Bedford
Alan Bird
Dean Bird
Bas Blackbourn BEM
Sheila Blanchard
Marjorie Blatherwick
Mr R C Bloodsworth
Audrey and Gordon Bolton
David G Brewster
Steven John Broad
M Bromfield
Anthony J Brown
Rodger Brownlow
Mrs Gillian Bryant
Mrs Dorothy Buckingham
Mrs S B Butters
P G D Byllam-Barnes
Rodney E Callow
Colin Carr
Thomas Herbert Chafer MA
Miss E M Chester
Mr J F Clark
R Alan Clark
Ranald W M Clouston
Robert G Cockerham
Timothy Cockerill
Lieutenant E C Coleman RN
Major (retd) Brett Collier
Martin and Elfrida Cordeaux
Sir Patrick Cormack FSA MP
Blandford W Coulbeck
Henry G Coutanche
Frank S Cox
Rosemary M Crust
Paul De Maeyer

Peter K Dennis
Mr and Mrs Ralph E Dickinson
Margaret Diggle
Diana M Dixon, DL
Jennifer Dixon née Cade
Doncaster Library and Information Services
Dr and Mrs H M Drake
Ernest Arthur Duffin
Eric C W Dunham
Ian Langton Durham
Marjorie Eassom
Ray Elliott
Charles Christopher Ellis
M F H English
Peter Fairweather
H B Fenning
Mr A E Fillingham
B Fletcher
Peter D Fletcher
Jennifer A Foster
Rodney A Foster
Mrs A E Fox
T A Foye
Martin Frisby-Boor
Frith, Denis A
Prince Yuri Galitzine
Len Gaunt
Peter Clifford Gawith
Andrew G Gledhill
Derek and Jean Godson
P R Graham
Peter Derek Gray
Doris Greenslade
B and W Gresham
Z Grice
Bryan Hall
Michael Hanna
R E Hardy
Brian Haworth
Michael Lynton Haycraft
Hilary Healey
P D Hemphrey
Heritage Trust of Lincolnshire
Miss Elizabeth Hill
G F Horton
Joan M Hoult

Nicholas John Howard
Mrs B M Jackson
Edward Jackson
Mr and Mrs Antony Jarvis
Miss K D Johnson
David Kaye
Ted Keal
Garth Anthony Ketteringham
Dr Charles Kightly
Winston Kime
Mr and Mrs N G Kirkman
A and Y J Lacy
Mr and Mrs Brian Lamb
Rita Larder
Gordon W Lauder
John D Leefe OBE
Mr and Mrs G A Lewis, Spalding
R John Linell
P and L Lyon
Bridget Makins
Miss Hilda Mason
Mrs Linda Mason
Mick and Margaret Medcalf
Chris Medley
Joan Lesley Milsom (née Hudson)
Miss F A R Murray OBE, MA BSc(Econ)
John R Needham
Joan Nelson
Merrilie Nicholson
Rosemary M Oliver
Elizabeth O'Neill
Jean E A Ostrowski
Joyce E Payne
James W Peat
Brian Peeps
Mrs Nancy Pepperdine
Lesley Pinchbeck
John Neville Porter
D W J Price Esq
Mr and Mrs J Pritchard
Philip Race
Marion Rance
David M Robertson
Phyllis M Robinson
Mrs E B Robson
Shelagh H Rogers
Susan Jane Rushby
Sandra M A Sardeson
Mrs Henrietta Schultka

Sandra and Richard Sendall
Paul Shillito
Sibthorp Library, Bishop Grosseteste College
Heather Y Simpson
Joyce Skinner CBE
Harry Sleaford
Michael M Sleight
Christopher John Sorby
Councillor W J Speechley CBE FRSA
Mr John Michael Stead
David Steele
Alan and Sue Stennett
Michael and Mary Stevens
Emerson Stone
M A Storer
Mr and Mrs M Stracey
Edward Swann
Mr E G Taylor
John D Taylor CBE
Michael Laurence Tebbutt
Michael and Elizabeth Thomas
Mr M W Trickett
John R Twigg
Doreen M Tyson
Elizabeth A Valley
Ronald A Vincent
Mary Wainwright
Jane Ward
S Warmoth, Grimsby
Mrs Eileen Warren
Susan Watkin
R J Watts
Lance Vincent Waumsley
J M Westcombe
P Wheatley
John William White
The Revd John Wickstead
H B Williams
Rt Hon Lady Willoughby de Eresby
Mrs Celia Wilson
Mr A R J and Mrs M A Winn
Eric Woods
Miss C H Wray

In addition, the author and publisher wish to thank those subscribers who also kindly supported this publication but did not wish for their names to be recorded in this list.